Teaching/Learning Anti-Racism

A DEVELOPMENTAL APPROACH

Teaching/Learning Anti-Racism

A DEVELOPMENTAL APPROACH

*Louise Derman-Sparks and
Carol Brunson Phillips*

FOREWORD BY ASA G. HILLIARD, III

Teachers College, Columbia University
New York and London

Published by Teachers College Press, 1234 Amsterdam Avenue, New York, NY 10027

Library of Congress Cataloging-in-Publication Data

Derman-Sparks, Louise.
    Teaching/learning anti-racism : a developmental approach / Louise
Derman-Sparks and Carol Brunson Phillips ; foreword by Asa G.
Hilliard III.
        p.   cm.
    Includes bibliographical references and index.
    ISBN 0-8077-3638-4 (cloth : alk. paper). —ISBN 0-8077-3637-6
(pbk. : alk. paper)
    1. Racism—Study and teaching.   I. Phillips, Carol Brunson.
II. Title.
HT1506.D47   1997
305.8'007'1—dc21   97-18761

ISBN 0-8077-3637-6 (paper)
ISBN 0-8077-3638-4 (cloth)

Printed on acid-free paper
Manufactured in the United States of America

04 03 02 01 00 99 98 97   8 7 6 5 4 3 2 1

To Robert and Burnece Brunson and Ann and Albert Robbins, who started us on the journey, and Douglass Sparks, Holly Sparks, and Brandon Fitzgerald Phillips, who carry it on

Anti-racism education is not an end in itself but rather the beginning of a new approach to thinking, feeling and acting.
—From the Introduction

Contents

Foreword

Racism has a history, causes, a structure, and consequences (Schwartz & Disch, 1970; Wobogo, 1976; Woodward, 1966). Dialogue about racism can be conducted with minimal information about these things, in which case there is often more heat than light. On the other hand, a study of the history, causes, structure, and consequences offers some hope that effective interventions may be developed to reverse the course of racism. However, because there is an important affective component to this study, good information may not be received.

It is virtually impossible to approach the study of racism dispassionately. Victims of racism harbor anger, frustration, impatience, and so forth. Perpetrators and beneficiaries of racist systems exhibit various forms of denial and other defenses. This is why the recognition of racism is rarely connected to an appropriate response at an appropriate level. For example, even though racism is endemic and has been so for the past few hundred years at least, a helping/healing discipline such as psychology offers minimal help in analysis or treatment. The *DSM* lists denial, delusions, projection, phobias, and distortion—all of which are aspects of racism—as psychological disorders, yet racist behavior is not identified as a mental illness.

The primary form of racism is White supremacy. This is much more than the more trivial stereotyping and prejudice or human relations issues. White-supremacy activities go far beyond the interpersonal frictions based on race. White supremacy is a *structured system* of belief and behavior (Feagin & Vera, 1995). This system can be seen in real estate redlining, de jure or de facto segregation in schools, media slander, and the misuse of academic power (Guthrie, 1976; Lutz & Collins, 1993; Herrnstein & Murray, 1994). Because of the structural nature of White supremacy, an effective remedy for it must be structured at its base. The structure of White supremacy is a matter of both belief and behavior embedded within systems.

Racism and/or white supremacy depend on the construct "race," which has been given *scientific* legitimacy only during the past three centuries (Barzun, 1965; Gossett, 1973; Montagu, 1942). That construct has taken on a life of its own, becoming a substitute in many cases for the more traditional basis of group identity, culture. The greed of the slavery, colonialism, apartheid, and ideology of White-supremacy structures, coupled with the fear of competition and retaliation from victims of the system, has fed the hardening of the structure. Therefore, we have two fundamental problems. On the one hand, we have the problem of causes (fear and greed). On the other hand we have the problem of structures of domination. Any lasting response to racism, any anti-racism response, must respond to both of these.

A part of the response is conceptual and historical awareness. Another part is to develop an insight into affect and behaviors of individuals and groups within the larger structured system. Yet another response is to understand the politics and economics of the system and to respond to these.

Given the depth and complicated nature of the problem, it is a wonder that anyone would charge into the cauldron, motivated by hope, respect for humanity, and a profound valuing of justice. But that is exactly what we see here. Two colleagues and friends, who began their quest many years ago, chose to confront issues in an intensive way in an educational setting, with their students. From modest beginnings, they have developed greater sophistication. Their sophistication is a consequence of reading and dialogue, but most important of all, it is a consequence of human encounters over real behaviors. The anecdotal materials presented here bring a needed discipline to mere theorizing. By grounding theory in experience, Carol Brunson Phillips and Louise Derman-Sparks have given us a valuable longitudinal case study of intervention.

Having known both of these wonderful people for virtually the whole time they have been engaged in this project, I marvel at their courage, tenacity, perception, and openness, and their basic love of human beings. It is much easier to leave this problem alone. Who needs the tension, the disappointment, the frustration, the conflicts? Only those who have hope and who are committed to erasing the evil force of racism, without compromise, could persist.

The authors have offered us enlightenment, potential directions for action, and a level of hope. I do not know if the virus of racism/White supremacy can be eliminated. I believe that if it can, it will be in large measure because of the type of work presented here.

Asa G. Hilliard, III
Fuller E. Callaway Professor of Urban Education
Georgia State University

REFERENCES

Barzun, J. (1965). *Race: A study in superstition.* New York: Harper.

Feagin, J. R., & Vera, H. (1995). *White racism: The basics.* Routledge: New York.

Gossett, T. F. (1973). *Race: The history of an idea in America.* New York: Schoken.

Guthrie, R. (1976). *Even the rat was white.* New York: Harper and Row.

Herrnstein, R. J., & Murray, C. (1994). *The bell curve: Intelligence and class structure in American life.* New York: Free Press.

Lutz, C. A., & Collins, J. L. (1993). *Reading National Geographic*. Chicago: University of Chicago Press.

Montague, A. (1942). *Man's most dangerous myth: The fallacy of race*. New York: Columbia University Press.

Schwartz, B., & Disch, R. (1970). *White racism: Its history, pathology and practice*. New York: Dell.

Wobogo, V. (1976). Diop's two cradle theory and the origin of white racism. *Black Books Bulletin, 4*(4), pp. 20–37.

Woodward, C. V. (1966). *The strange career of Jim Crow*. New York: Oxford.

Preface

The context in which we grow up and in which we carry out our professional lives influences how all of us teach, across all subjects. Doing anti-racism education particularly engages us at the deepest personal level, as it does our students. Therefore, knowing a little about the two of us will help you, the reader, understand where we began.

I (Carol Brunson Phillips) am a native of Chicago where I lived until I finished school and began my professional work in early childhood education.

Throughout my career, I have been involved in both teaching young children and training teachers, first as a teacher of 4-year-olds and instructor of child development at Prairie State College in Illinois, and then as a member of the Human Development Faculty at Pacific Oaks College in Pasadena, specializing in early childhood education and cultural influences on development. At present, I am the executive director of the Council for Early Childhood Professional Recognition, a Washington, D.C.–based national association that conducts projects to increase the status and recognition of early childhood education professionals.

Two underlying themes characterize both my work and my life—the commitment to young children and the commitment to the integrity of the developing human being. Both have roots in a long line of African American ancestry that deeply embeds me in family loyalty and standing up for what is right.

I (Louise Derman-Sparks) grew up in Brooklyn and Manhattan, in a working-class Jewish family where social activism was a way of life. My desire to become a teacher appeared early and remained persistent. My mother relates that my dramatic play as a young child revolved around teacher roles, rather than more domestic ones. As a high school student in the fifties, I became part of the folk music scene and, in college, made my debut as an activist by joining anti–nuclear bomb testing and civil rights activities of the early sixties. Involvement in various social justice causes remains an active theme in my life.

Becoming an early childhood teacher in 1963, I first worked for the Perry Preschool Project, and then the Piaget-based Ypsilanti Early Childhood Project. These experiences opened my eyes to the dangers of a "cultural deprivation" approach, as well as to the enormous potential early childhood education offered to young children and families living in poverty, if it proceeded from an anti-racist base.

Coming to Pacific Oaks College in 1974, where I am still on the faculty, I embarked on my career as an adult educator. In 1980, I also began the research that led to initiating the Anti-Bias Education Task Force in 1985, and in 1989, publication of *Anti-Bias Curriculum: Tools for Empowering Young Children* (Derman-Sparks and the ABC Task Force, 1989). Since then I continue to focus on the complex challenge of preparing adults to meaningfully and effectively use an anti-bias approach in their work as early childhood educators.

When we began our journey together as anti-racism educators, we each had some previous experience in the civil rights movement of the sixties, and a deep commitment, but knew very little about what one-on-one anti-racism education would entail. The first few semesters, we often felt as if the process controlled us rather than the other way around. We learned as much, if not more, from our failures as we did from our successes. Gradually, through close attention to both students and our own responses, constant dialogue with ourselves and colleagues, and much reading, we gained in skill, understanding, and confidence. As we faced and resolved many of the personal tensions racism provokes in ourselves and saw that at least some of our students would change, we were able to relax and to accept the joys as well as the difficulties of anti-racism teaching.

Our work on the manuscript for this book has evolved over a period of 15 years. We wrote our first draft in 1981, with support from a Mina Shaughnessy Grant awarded by the U.S. Department of Education, Fund for the Improvement of Post Secondary Education. However, we did not complete the final manuscript until the nineties, although we never stopped working with anti-racism education in a variety of settings.

Several considerations led to our decision to return to and complete our initial draft. First, the need for anti-racism education among educators and other human service professionals remains critical. Second, the lessons we learned remain equally relevant today. Our work still uses the same conceptual framework, goals, and pedagogical principles, although, over the years, we have modified or added specific content and activities in response to new societal conditions and groups of learners. Updates and adaptations will always be a necessary component of effective anti-racism education. Third, since we completed our first draft, other educators and psychologists (e.g., William Cross, Janet Helms, and Beverely Daniel Tatum) published their thinking about racial identity development, placing our observations and analyses of the progression of student growth in a broader context. Fourth, reading what others had written about anti-racism training helped us decide that what we had to say about facilitating the process would be a useful contribution.

We began as fledglings. Many years later, we are still learning.

Acknowledgments

This book has had a long gestation time and many people helped it along the way to its birth. We thank them all. In addition, we particularly want to recognize:

The Mina Shaughnessy Scholars Program of the Fund for the Improvement of Post Secondary Education at the U.S. Department of Education, which provided the initial spark and support for us as practitioners to write about our work

The Council for Early Childhood Professional Recognition for providing a constant backdrop of support

The faculty writing group at Pacific Oaks College who urged us on

Betty Jones, who insisted the gestation period had gone on long enough

George Gonzales, Edward Greene, and Yolanda Torres, with whom we created the first version of our anti-racism course

Elizabeth Ashley, Antonia Darder, Lynda Doi Ficke, and Joyce Robinson, who contributed to the fine-tuning of the course while teaching with one of us in the later years

Shelagh Mullings, Vivienne Oxford, Kathy Spencer, and Rhonda Williams, who, respectively, typed and managed us through the first, subsequent, and final drafts of the manuscript

Jim Kendrick, who with skill and humor helped us craft the final version

Francie Kendall, whose valuable feedback and encouragement made a big difference

Rheta Negrete Karwin, who looked through the final version with the eyes of the audience we want to reach and kept the office fires going while Louise wrote

Cecelia Alvarado and Phyllis Brady, with whom the journey continues

Vicki Frelow, Luba Lynch, Marilyn Segal, and Valora Washington, whose belief in the importance of anti-bias work has made it possible to keep going

Bill Sparks, who, as many times before, took on more than his share of home and family duties when deadlines pressed and always provided love and nurturing

J. D. Andrews, who removed obstacles and cleared away barriers as only he could have done

Finally, we especially thank our students, who took up the challenge of facing racism with courage and persistence and from whom we learned what it means to teach carefully.

Teaching/Learning Anti-Racism

A DEVELOPMENTAL APPROACH

Introduction

Why does this class affect people so much? I think it's because in untying the knot of racism, we're unraveling the brainwashing each of us experienced growing up. This has had a dehumanizing toll, and in unraveling even a bit of the whole, we feel tremendously excited. We have only to unravel further to reclaim ourselves more completely.

—Cathy Berger, Letter to authors

This book is about a course we co-taught for 10 years to undergraduate and graduate students enrolled at Pacific Oaks College in California. Our aim is to describe the process that evolves as teachers and students grapple with the complexities and challenges of learning about racism and becoming anti-racist. We have combined methodology and course content descriptions with student writings and our analyses of student growth. In addition, we discuss the personal challenges and feelings that we faced, seek to convey the dynamics of an extraordinary teaching/learning process, and suggest specific pedagogical tools.

How best to address racism and anti-racism in a course is one of the first issues confronting educators. A parable that we often use to begin our first class highlights the dilemma:

Once upon a time a woman, strolling along a riverbank, hears a cry for help and seeing a drowning person rescues him. She no sooner finishes administering artificial respiration when another cry requires another rescue. Again, she has only just helped the second person when a third call for help is heard. After a number of rescues, she begins to realize that she is pulling some people out of the river more than once. By this time the rescuer is exhausted and resentful, feeling that if people are stupid or careless enough to keep landing in the river, they can rescue themselves. She is too annoyed, tired, and frustrated to look around her.

Shortly after, another woman walking along the river hears the cries for help and begins rescuing people. She, however,

1

wonders why so many people are drowning in this river. Looking around her, she sees a hill where something seems to be pushing people off. Realizing this as the source of the drowning problem, she is faced with a difficult dilemma: If she rushes uphill, people presently in the river will drown; if she stays at the river pulling them out, more people will be pushed in. What can she do?

Some think a solution is impossible. Yet if we define racism as the force pushing people into the water, then this tale metaphorically suggests three alternative perspectives for educators and human service practitioners: (1) Rescue people in trouble and return them to the conditions that caused the problem; (2) after rescuing people teach them how to manage their problems so that if they "get pushed into the river again" they at least won't drown; and (3) organize with people to destroy the source of the problem.

We opt for the third position, for professional training should do more than teach people to respond to the symptoms or consequences of oppressive conditions. Rather, it must help people develop strategies for responding to the source of racism, and encourage people to reevaluate their own role in its continuation. In other words, anti-racism education is about learning to understand and to eliminate the problem on the hill. Our parable illustrates the dilemma of failing to have a comprehensive view of the source and consequences of racism, as well as of the role of individuals in either continuing racism or transforming it by their choice of action strategy.

RACISM AND ANTI-RACISM

We define racism as an institutionalized system of economic, political, social, and cultural relations that ensures that one racial group has and maintains power and privilege over all others in all aspects of life. Individual participation in racism occurs when the objective outcome of behavior reinforces these relations, regardless of the subjective intent. Consequently, an individual may act in a racist manner unintentionally.

In the United States, Whites are automatically considered members of the dominant group, and people of color, including Asian-Pacific Americans, Blacks, Latinos, and Native Americans, are automatically considered members of the subordinate or dominated group. The individual's relationship to racism is defined by group membership; so too are his or her responsibilities for anti-racism.

In a racist society an ideology of racism—a system of beliefs, attitudes, and symbols constructed and legitimized by those with political and cultural power—socializes each succeeding generation. Consideration of the psychological impact of racist ideology on the development of Whites and people of color also suggests specific issues that anti-racism education must address. In particular, the dynamics of internalized superiority, on the one hand, and internalized oppression, on the other, must be uncovered, examined, and transformed. Anti-racist consciousness and behavior can be learned and lived, as the Americans of all backgrounds who have actively challenged racism throughout our history demonstrate.

Anti-racism education is not an end in itself but rather the beginning of a new approach to thinking, feeling, and acting. Anti-racist consciousness and behavior means having the self-awareness, knowledge, and skills—as well as the confidence, patience, and persistence—to challenge, interrupt, modify, erode, and eliminate any and all manifestations of racism within one's own spheres of influence. It requires vision and will, an analysis of racism's complexities and changing forms, and an understanding of how it affects people socially and psychologically.

Racism affects everyone, and so, too, anti-racism education benefits everyone. However, because the structural relationship to racism differs for Whites and for people of color, the specific issues and steps in becoming anti-racist also differ. People of color learn how not to collude in their own oppression; Whites learn how not to be oppressors. The characteristics of an anti-racist identity for people of color include—

- Greater understanding of and sense of security in their own racial/ethnic identity
- The ability to view both their group and other racial/ethnic groups more objectively
- Being actively anti-racist within their own spheres of influence, which involves establishing meaningful relationships with Whites who acknowledge and are respectful of their self-definition, and building coalitions with members of other oppressed groups

For Whites, anti-racist identity includes

- New understanding and internalization of a realistic White racial identity and a new sense of their cultural identity
- Remaining open to and searching for new information as they engage in on-going self-examination of their participation in racism
- The ability to work effectively in multiracial settings and be actively anti-racist within their own sphere of influence (Tatum, 1995)

ORIGINS AND EVOLUTION OF OUR ANTI-RACISM COURSE

The origins of our course in anti-racism education were in the 1970s at Pacific Oaks College. Despite the institution's commitment to "honoring the uniqueness in each person," we were dissatisfied with our students' preparation for effectively teaching children of color. Pacific Oak's philosophy of "color blindness," combined with a heavy emphasis on individual development, excluded other crucial components of children's development and early childhood education—namely, the impact of culture and racism. Together with Edward Greene and Yolanda Torres, we created and, for the first semester, all taught a new course we called "School, Family and Community Interaction in a Pluralistic Society." Unsure of how students would receive it, we circulated a flyer explaining the new course and asking, "Are you ready for this?"

There were four goals of the framework for curriculum content, activities, and evaluation criteria. We wanted students to—

1. *Deepen self-knowledge* by developing racial and cultural identity; recognizing their attitudes, beliefs, and behaviors toward others; and understanding the impact of racism on their own development
2. *Acquire a new information base* by understanding the dynamics of institutional and cultural racism in general and, in particular, how racism affects the mission, polices, structure, and methods of education and human service programs
3. *De-center and extend empathy* by gaining awareness, knowledge, and appreciation of the cultural realities, life experiences, and history of individuals and groups different from their own racial and ethnic background
4. *Become activists* by developing skills and confidence to be change agents in work and community settings

Over several semesters and numerous modifications of the course, our approach evolved. Class by class, we tried out activities, observed students' response, and then spent hours together figuring out what happened, what did not happen, and what we should do next, in light of our goals. Some insights came earlier than others. For example, when an emotional explosion occurred among the students during the fourth or fifth week in a class, we planned changes in the structure of the next semester's class so it would not happen again. But it did. And after several tries, we realized that the explosion was a necessary part of the process and stopped trying to avoid it. Instead, we worked at honing our skills for dealing with it and learned that emotion, as well as cognition, is necessary and to be embraced. Students' journals (a course requirement to encourage documentation and self-dialogue) also became a key source for our education as teachers. This book reflects a constellation of many experiences over several semesters, although it is written as if it took place during a one-semester class.

We worked with approximately 200 students over the years. They ranged in age from 25 to 60 years old and were European American, African American, Latin American, and Asian American. The students were preparing to be early childhood, elementary, and community college teachers; marriage/family/children counselors; parent educators; and school administrators. As we worked with them we discovered many things about how to make such a class effective.

Our most significant lesson was the discovery that the construction of anti-racist identity, consciousness, and behavior is a transformative rather than a linear process. Students' growth revealed identifiable and qualitatively different phases. This notion, startlingly new to us at the time, although since identified and explored by several other educators and psychologists (see Chapter 2), had critical implications for the evolving organization and pedagogy of our course.

Students' uncovering of contradictions—between their stated principles and practice, between inherited ideas and new information, between self-image and feedback from others—sparked the search for new ways to think and act. This search motivated continued learning. Our role as teachers reflected this dialectic process. A delicate interaction between challenge and support stimulates the search and thus facilitates students' learning. Yet, the teacher as guide is at the same time a learner because he or she must pay attention to each student's rhythm of growth.

ORGANIZATION OF THE BOOK

This book is organized in three parts. Part I describes the conceptual framework for anti-racism and the premises underlying our pedagogy. We explore the structural and ideological components of racism (Chapter 1) and the relationships of the individual to racism and anti-racism (Chapter 2).

Part II (Chapters 3–6) describes the course Racism and Human Development and details how each class session contributes to the progression of students' growth to anti-racist identity, consciousness, and behavior. Each chapter's focus is on one of the four major developmental phases of student growth, and within each chapter we describe (1) teaching challenges, (2) activities and teaching strategies, and (3) analyses of students' growth, illustrated by excerpts from the journals they were required to write throughout the course.

Finally, Part III (Chapter 7) discusses ways to make the course your own. Topics include (1) reflections on generic issues related to our role as anti-racism educators, (2) factors to consider when adapting the course to different settings, students, and social-political dynamics, and (3) suggestions for continuing self-education.

There are several ways to read this book. If you are a person who likes to familiarize yourself with the authors' theoretical framework, you should begin with Part I. If you prefer to plunge right into the firsthand account of the course and find the theoretical material more useful afterward, then go right to Part II. If you want to know what the entire sequence of the course looked like, read the "Teaching Challenges" and "Activities" sections of Chapters 3–6 before reviewing the "Student Responses." If you seek a sense of the students' entire journey, read the "Student Responses" in each chapter, without interruption from the sections dealing with the curriculum. As you use the book to teach an anti-racism course, you will probably want to get a sense of the whole, read additional books to strengthen your knowledge base, pay particular attention to Part III, and reread specific chapters, or sections of chapters, as the course progresses.

A note about style: Terms referring to racial/ethnic identity groups are capitalized to show respect to all groups. However, for the term "people of color," which we use as a generic noun to collectively refer to groups targeted by racism, we follow the convention of not using capitals.

A FINAL WORD

Teachers face the same contradictions that racism creates for our students. Their struggle to become and live as anti-racists is ours as well. Over the years, we have also come to know and greatly benefit from the work and support of other anti-racism educators. None of us can do anti-racism education work in isolation. It is too complex. It requires multiple voices in dialogue and struggle, and emotional support from people who understand its demands and help us keep growing. There are also wonderful rewards. When a student writes, "This class has accomplished so much in the freeing of my soul," it is worth all the hard work. Becoming anti-racist strengthens our humanity—restoring and redirecting energy for growth in ourselves and for participating in the humanizing and freeing of our country.

PART I

A Conceptual Framework for Racism and Anti-Racism

This first part of this book describes the core concepts about racism that underlie our model of anti-racism education and our work as anti-racism educators. Chapter 1 addresses structural and ideological components. Chapter 2 focuses on the role of the individual and the developmental journey to anti-racist identity, consciousness, and behavior.

Many excellent books are cited as references in the chapters. We refer educators and other readers to these, for they uncover the complexities and provide illustrative historic and current data about the issues and assumptions we touch on only briefly.

CHAPTER 1

The Dynamics of Racism

The very first thing we need to do as a nation and as individual members of society is to confront our past. . . . We need to recognize it for what it was and is and not explain away, excuse it, or justify it. Having done that, we should then make a good faith effort to turn our history around so that we can see it in front of us, so that we can avoid doing what we have done for so long.
—*John Hope Franklin,* The Color Line

Racism is an institutionalized system of power. It encompasses a web of economic, political, social, and cultural structures, actions, and beliefs that systemize and ensure an unequal distribution of privilege, resources, and power in favor of the dominant racial group and at the expense of all other racial groups. A system of subordination is thus created and perpetuated (Hilliard, 1992). Further, the outcome of individual, cultural, and institutional policies and actions, rather than the intent behind them, determines the presence of racism. Lack of intentionality, or knowledge, in a given situation does not change objective consequences for people of color. While most Whites believe there is no racism if there is no intent to judge by race, "from the perspective of the recipients of racism, the expressed intention is relatively unimportant in comparison with the results"(Stroup & Fleming, 1995, p. 31).

In the United States, we see racism organizing all aspects of life. An ideology constructed by the dominant group justifies and normalizes the systemic inequality and places blame for it on the shoulders of those it excludes. Consequently, racist relationships are not an aberration but, rather, a part of the basic fabric of normal life of American society. To one degree or another, everyone is enmeshed in this systemic web, for there are no bystanders or neutral observers (Hilliard, Jenkins, & Scott, 1979). Ultimately, "racism is the deepest level of hurt that can be placed on a society" (Hilliard, 1992, p. 7). Our approach to anti-racism education begins with this understanding.

In this chapter, we discuss racism's forms, the principles by which it is maintained, and its ideological components. We conclude the chapter with a discussion of the changing face of racism—how the ideology is being updated to prevail in a changing social, economic, and legal environment.

INSTITUTIONAL, CULTURAL, AND
INDIVIDUAL FORMS OF RACISM

Racism operates in three forms: institutional, cultural, and individual. The three forms interact and reinforce one another.

Institutional racism includes the mission, policies, organizational structures, and behaviors built into all institutional systems and services. Although these components usually reinforce each other, contradictions among them sometimes open up potential windows for action. For example, the education system's policies and practices that reproduce the power relationships of racism (and of class and gender as well) conflict with the espoused mission of public schools to provide equal access to all children. In early childhood education, the use of developmental theories that are implicitly grounded in a European and European American cultural perspective contradicts the professional mandate to meet the needs of all children and families.

Cultural racism consists of the beliefs, symbols, and underlying cultural rules of behavior that teach and endorse the superiority of the dominant American culture (an amalgam of English and other western European cultures). Although in daily life, cultural racism can feel as natural or invisible as the air, it reflects the ideology of the dominant group with an identifiable structure and practice (Dominelli, 1992). Cultural racism plays a critical role in socializing individuals to participate in and maintain institutional racism.

Individual racism consists of attitudes and behaviors that carry out and maintain the power relationships of racism. While such individual acts may appear to be specific to the person carrying them out, they are fueled by and reflect the institutional and cultural dimensions of racism. Individual racism is more than being prejudiced or holding stereotypes of specific groups.

> An individual's personal racial prejudices are transformed into racism by becoming linked to the power of societal systems. . . . Because of this linkage, . . . prejudices [that] might otherwise be limited to hurtful and ugly behavior in . . . private encounters becomes a . . . destructive instrument with far greater scope. (Barndt, 1991, p. 53)

To highlight this point, many anti-racism educators use the shorthand definition: Racism equals racial prejudice plus institutional power.

Understanding the dynamics and interactions between these three major forms of racism helps identify collective political strategies as well as individual actions that are necessary to eliminate racism. For, just as individual educators and human service practitioners "should not be scapegoated for structural inadequacies," individuals do have the responsibility for changing their own behavior as well as working with others to tackle organizational and societal policy and practice (Dominelli, 1992, p. 170).

It is the subtle presence of racism in our normal activities, coupled with our failure to make the connections between the personal, institutional and cultural levels of racism, which make it so hard for White people to recognize its existence in their particular behavior and combat it effectively. (Dominelli, 1992, p. 165)

Further, identifying these forms of racism helps us to explain principles that govern the structural dynamics of racism.

THE STRUCTURAL DYNAMICS OF RACISM

Our conceptual framework draws on four principles that drive the overall dynamics of racism in the United States:

1. Racism operates both overtly and covertly.
2. Racism is based on a politically constructed concept of race.
3. The U.S. manifestation of racism is rooted in the developmental capitalism and colonialism that Europeans cultivated in the New World.
4. Racism interacts in complex ways with sexism and classism.

Overt and Covert Manifestations

All forms of racism operate both overtly and covertly, the latter having particular significance for anti-racism education. Overt manifestations are fairly easy to distinguish. They consist of policies and practices that openly maintain the right of White privilege and openly exclude people of color. Former "Jim Crow" laws exemplify overt institutional racism. The multitude of books purporting to prove the biological inferiority of African Americans and other people of color illustrate overt cultural racism. Choosing to join the Ku Klux Klan (KKK) or other explicitly White supremacist groups reflects overt individual racism.

Covert racism is harder to identify. It includes all those institutional policies and practices whose habitual outcome is inequitable relationships between Whites and people of color, even when "race" is not an explicit or even an intended factor. In education, practices such as IQ testing, tracking, a lack of understanding about differences in cultural learning styles, curriculum materials centered on Euro-American culture, and ineffective bilingual education all create unequal educational opportunity and foster outcomes that maintain the status quo of institutional racism. Moreover, teachers who consider themselves nonracist because they do not hold overtly bigoted beliefs carry out these practices.

The deep roots and strength of covert racism became increasingly apparent in the 1980s and 1990s, as the ending of overt legal racism only scratched the surface of the underlying structural power relationships between Whites and people of color. Further, human service and educational programs are particularly vulnerable to covert racism, requiring educators to develop skills similar to those of a detective—digging below the surface and uncovering subtle beliefs, behaviors, and assumptions.

Political Construct

Racism is based on a politically constructed concept of race. The notion of race as a determining factor in human behavior and ability has no scientific basis. Nevertheless, as a sociopolitical construct, it remains very real in terms of the treatment people receive in all aspects of their lives.

In the United States, skin color predominately defines race, with a variety of other genetic, behavioral, and moral characteristics connected to each racial group. People with White skin, who trace their origins to Europe, are considered members of the dominant group; Asian-Pacific Americans, Blacks, Latinos, and Native Americans are considered members of "minority" or subordinate groups. We use the term *people of color* to refer to all the groups placed in the subordinate structural position. Legal power to determine racial group categories and membership is in the hands of the dominant group in a society, rather than up for individual choice. Moreover,

> far from being static or fixed, race as an oppressive concept within social relations is fluid and ever-changing. . . . That which is termed "Black", "Hispanic" or "Oriental" by those in power to describe one human being's "racial background" in a particular setting can have little historic or practical meaning within another social formation. (Marable, 1995, p. 186)

Legislation in the 17th and 18th centuries defined the concept of "whiteness" in the United States by melting the various immigrant European ethnic groups into a single "race" defined by skin color (Gossett, 1963). The legal boundaries of "Negro" shifted several times, reflecting changing economic and political needs of Whites. For example, in Virginia, in 1879, a Black person was defined as possessing one-fourth or more of "Negro blood"; by 1910, one-sixteenth or more Negro blood; and by 1930, any person with any ascertainable Negro blood was treated as a "colored" person (Franklin, 1993). Similar political gymnastics occupied legislatures in most other states and at the federal level as well.

From the beginning, the core racial distinction in the United States focused on White versus Black. (This does not imply that other groups have not also been severely oppressed by racism in the United States.) However, this biracial framework is undergoing considerable transformation in the 1990s as population demographics change and Latinos and Asian-Pacific Americans become a larger portion of the people of color in the United States (Marable, 1995).

Finally, it is important to understand that our society confuses the concepts of race and ethnicity. In the United States, "Americans generally make few distinctions between 'ethnicity' and 'race,' and the two concepts are usually used interchangeably" (Marable, 1995, p. 186). We believe that each refers to very different aspects of human identity, and that the distinctions are significant. "Race" has a very political meaning, playing a key role in determining how people are treated in our society. "Ethnicity," which refers to the geographic place of origin of an individual's family and group identity, can give us a historical framework to understand an individual's cultural context. Blurring the distinctions between the two terms reflects a profound misunderstanding and/or denial of racism as an institutionalized system of privilege and power. When educators and human service practitioners use "race" and "ethnicity" interchangeably, they confuse the positive role of culture in human development and daily life with the negative impact of racism.

Origins in Developing Capitalism

Racism in the United States originated in the developing capitalism and European colonial expansion of the 15th century and, more specifically, in the formation and evolution of capitalism in American society. In the "New World" of North and South America, enslaved labor played a key role in the process of developing capitalism and colonial expansion. Slavery was not a new idea, but the form slavery took in the New World set the stage for the racism with which we are saddled today, where "a slave ceased to be regarded as a person at all" (Institute of Race Relations, 1982, p. 24).

In the United States, the colonization and robbing of flourishing Native American civilization, the importation of Africans as slaves, the expropriation of the land of Mexicans in the Southwest, and the exploitation of Asian labor in the building of railroads and mining of gold combined to lay the economic, political, and ideological foundation for the present structural relationships of racism (Takaki, 1993). The Constitution itself reflected the acceptance that people other than Whites were not fully human—originally containing the provision that representation and taxes were to be appropriated according to numbers determined by adding free persons (i.e., Whites) and three-fifths of all other persons, which included Black slaves and Native Americans.

Knowledge of the formation and history of racism in the United States is essential: The deep roots of its core structures continue to nurture current forms of racism (Jordan, 1974). However, throughout U.S. history, economic, political, and cultural contradictions also created fissures, opening up possibilities for challenging racism (Aptheker, 1993). Even while the Constitution was a key political building block in the creation of systemic racism, the Declaration of Independence and the Bill of Rights provided tools for questioning racism's basic tenets. Necessities of industrialization as well as moral and political opposition underlay the ending of slavery. Religious beliefs undergird justifications of racism while also energizing resistance.

Interaction with Classism and Sexism

While central to the formation, history, and current realities of U.S. society, racism began and continues to exist in a complex interaction with the systemic dynamics of class and gender oppression. Considerable, sometimes heated, disagreement about the relationship of race, class, and gender exists in the literature. In particular, argument revolves around questions as to which of these institutional forms of oppression is primary, that is, from an evolutionary standpoint "which came first." Our approach derives from analyses that argue for the centrality of racism, while also acknowledging the critical roles of class and gender oppression in the politics of American society (Davis, 1983; Roediger, 1991). Thus, we contend that, while all Whites automatically have institutionalized privilege, they do not equally reap its benefits. Class, gender, and sexual orientation, along with other aspects of identity (including disability and age), influence how much and in what ways individuals experience and gain from their "whiteness." While all people of color are targeted by racism, the factors of class, gender, and sexual orientation also influence the ways and layers in which oppression occurs. The use of race to divide people with shared interests based on gender or class and thereby weaken their ability to resist exploitation is an ongoing theme in U.S. history (Davis, 1983; Zinn, 1980).

Ideological formulations justifying oppression based on gender and class also share key similarities with those justifying racism. Thus sexism

> involves the denigration of an entire people, this time on the basis of gender; justifications for this have included insistence on marked mental inferiority as well as decided temperamental inadequacies. Research occupying academicians in the 19th century also went to great lengths to prove the biological, inheritable inferiority of poor Whites, and that the poor are without merit, as well as without wealth, and that these absences are causally connected. (Aptheker, 1993, p. xv)

IDEOLOGICAL COMPONENTS: ASSUMPTIONS OF RACISM

Racist institutions not only create the structural conditions for racism, but also create a culturally sanctioned ideology that keeps the system operating. We now turn to a discussion of those core notions and their dynamics in the way people in the United States are socialized to live in a racist society.

Racist ideology is a set of notions that ascribe central importance to real or presumed biological, cultural, and psychological differences among racial groups, attributing the arrangement of both historic and current social systems to these differences. "It operates within the individual psyche and institutional structures of a society and legitimizes the domination and control by one group over others" (Hilliard et al., 1979, p. 79).

The underlying theme of all formulations of American racist ideology is the inferiority—genetic or cultural—of people of color. Glaring inequities in the distribution of wealth and power are then blamed on the inability of "inferior" groups to take advantage of the alleged democratic opportunities offered them. White privilege is justified without calling the system into question, thereby obscuring the actual dynamics of institutional policy, practices, and outcomes. While ideological and cultural arguments are the twin pillars supporting racism, one or the other may be in the forefront at any given time. Social policy of a particular historical era reflects the predominance of one or the other position.

The Biological Argument

Two fallacious assumptions form the linchpins of biologically based racist ideology:

1. Humans are classifiable into discrete, hierarchically ranked biological groups (with Whites at the top).
2. Differences among the races reflect the natural and/or ordained order and therefore are eternally fixed.

Since the 19th century, a number of scholars have provided in-depth analyses of the errors and manipulations of data by European and American physical and social scientists purporting to prove the truth of the above two assumptions (Gould, 1981). Rather than duplicate the wealth of documentation found in these critiques, we simply want to make the point that not only has biological inferiority or superiority never been proven, it has also been impossible to establish any biological criteria for defining race itself.

Despite the bankruptcy of biological approaches to justifying racism, the myth has not been deterred. Many people, if not most, have come to accept the concept of race as if it refers to an objective biological reality. Moreover, the social-policy consequences of the biological argument have been brutal to people of color. (See Chase, *The Legacy of Malthus* [1975], for hundreds of pages of evidence.) One well-publicized example is *The Bell Curve* (Herrnstein & Murray, 1994), which rehashed previous attempts to prove genetically inherited superior intelligence in Whites compared with Blacks. As Stephen Jay Gould (1995), an internationally respected expert on human evolution responded, "The mismeasure of man [and woman] continues, as a current bestseller revives the academic racism's old arguments" (p. 12). It is also worth noting that research for *The Bell Curve* was partly funded by the Pioneer Fund, an organization "founded on the belief in the superiority of White persons who settled in the original thirteen states" (Tucker, 1994, p. 194).

The Cultural Argument

"Blaming the victim" (Ryan, 1976) as a way of explaining the realities of the lives of people of color has become the most pervasive 20th-century version of the cultural inferiority argument. William Ryan's groundbreaking book (1976) defined blaming the victim as an ideological stance that locates the origins of social problems in the victims of the problem rather than in any deficiency or structural defect in the social system. Ryan identified four steps in the victim-blaming process:

1. Locate a social problem and population affected by it (e.g., African Americans, American Indians, and Latino Americans are more likely than European Americans to drop out of high school).
2. Compare the values and behaviors of the population affected by the social problem with the population that is not affected (e.g., White students).
3. Locate the source of the problem in how the affected population is different from the successful population (e.g., in their culture).
4. Initiate treatment that changes the affected population (eliminate use of their home language, change the family's child-rearing practices, teach them to act more like Whites).

Victim-blaming thus provides a framework for explaining the problems of people of color in our society without calling into question the institutionalized system of racial privilege. It is also used as a framework for developing strategies to ameliorate the problems of people of color without resorting to institutional change. Thus, it allows White people to remove themselves from complicity in the problem while thinking that they are doing something about it (Wellman, 1977).

Victim-blaming analysis is pervasive in educational and human service programs. Teachers, mental health professionals, and social workers who operate from a victim-blaming framework rarely see either the strengths of the people with whom they work or the real causes of the problems they are addressing. Rather, like the rescuer in the parable related in the Introduction, they see the persons calling for help as drowning simply because they do not know how to swim, and never look for what actually pushed them into the river in the first place.

The Legitimizing of Racist Ideology

As has been the case in the past, the production and dissemination of the ideology of racism in both its biological and cultural forms continue to hold the attention of physical and social scientists. In his critique of the role of American biological and social sciences in the creation of racist ideology and social policy, William Tucker (1994) clearly explains how the general public belief that "the operation of science was synonymous with the termination of politics made appeals to scientific authority a powerful strategy for influencing public policy" (p. 6). However, hiding behind the mantle of scientific "objectivity," "the effort to prove the innate intellectual inferiority of some groups has led *only* to oppressive and antisocial proposals; is has had no *other* use" (p. 8). For example, Lewis Terman, the father of the U.S. version of the IQ test—a continuing tool of racial oppression today—"insisted, that a 'less naive definition of . . . democracy . . . will have to square with the demonstrable facts of biological and psychological science'" (Tucker, 1994, p. 74).

Tucker's (1994) exhaustive critique of the science and politics of racial research leads him to the following conclusion:

> Although the obsession with racial differences has contributed absolutely nothing to our understanding of human intellectual processes, it has performed continuing service as support for political policies—and not benign ones. The imprimatur of science has been offered to justify, first, slavery and, later, segregation, nativism, sociopolitical inequality, class subordination, poverty, and the general futility of social and economic reform. (pp. 269–270)

Prescribing Social Reality

The ideology of racism prescribes the parameters for perceiving social reality, thereby defining guidelines for "desirable" interracial behavior. Once the members of a society are imbued with racist thinking, they will not only perceive their institutions as natural, they will also voluntarily carry out institutional mandates as if they are a function of their own individual choice.

However, if individuals become critical of the assumptions of racist ideology and reject its tenets, then racist institutional arrangements may no longer appear either natural or legitimate. The new frame of reference will produce a new perspective on society, human development, and one's own role—thereby creating a potential force for change. Anti-racism education must uncover and challenge the old ways of thinking, and foster these new ones.

Everyone born into American society learns the ideology of racism (although some are better students than others). All the socialization agents of society—families, schools, media, church, art, literature—contribute to this education. Messages bombard us all, ranging from the blatant to the subtle, from the macro to the micro, and from the written and spoken word to nonverbal behavioral interactions. Learning to think and behave according to the dictates of racist ideology—

1. Begins very early—probably by 2 years of age and most certainly by 3 and 4

2. Is imposed on children through a painful process of social conditioning about which they have no choice
3. Has harmful cognitive and emotional effects on the psychological development of both Whites and people of color (Clark, 1963; Dennis, 1981)

Oversimplified, and usually derogatory, notions about the traits and behaviors common to a specified group of people, and applied to each member of the group without regard to a person's individuality, characterize stereotypical thinking. Racial prejudice uses stereotypes about various racial and ethnic groups to pre-judge individuals and groups. Very early, children of all backgrounds learn stereotypes about other groups regardless of whether they have contact with actual people. Thus, stereotypes further shape a person's reality as they become filters through which to pre-judge and interpret the ideas and behavior of others.

Studies of the symbols that represent and communicate the messages of racist ideology highlight their power and pervasiveness. Chester Pierce (1980) suggests that the daily bombardment of these symbolic message has the same contaminating significance on an emotional, psychological level as trace elements and trace contaminants have on the physical level. He argues that "probably on any given day there will be, by a factor of millions, more of such subtle interactions than of gross, intentional violence" (1980, p. 250). Each one alone may not be noticeably harmful, but over time they become poisonous and very damaging. Awareness of these symbols' more covert and subtle forms is particularly important for educators.

NEW FACES OF RACISM

The legal ending of segregation in the 1960s and efforts at both the grass-roots and government levels initiated a major shift in the dynamics of racism in the United States. On the one hand, this led to some amelioration of conditions for people of color as evidenced by the emergence of a larger African American and Latino middle class; increased political representation at local, state, and national levels; and growth in the number of students of color entering higher education.

Yet many of these changes were more symbolic than real, revealing the strength of the deep structural rules that support the more covert forms of racism. For example, in 1994, White men still held 91.7% of all corporate officer positions and 88.1% of all director positions; people of color held 2.3% of all corporate officer and 5% of all director positions (Galen, with Palmer, 1994, p. 52). Moreover,

[e]ven those Blacks who moved . . . into the middle class averaged lower incomes than Whites of the same age and education. In absolute terms, they were much better

off than those they left behind, but relative to those they were competing with for jobs, they were still much worse. (Carnoy, 1994, p. 45)

African American mayors elected in major industrial cities found the economic base drastically eroded by the flight of industry to the suburbs and to other states and countries. Moreover, operating within the same institutional framework as previous mayors meant that many policies showed little difference from the earlier politics (Marable, 1995).

Changes in the economy and in regulatory laws beginning in the 1980s (e.g., tax benefits to people in the highest income brackets) resulted in an increase in the average income for people at the top 1% from $270,053 in 1977 to $484,566 in 1988. The average income of the lowest 10% fell from $4,113 to $3,504 (Franklin, 1993). This put the majority of people of color in an increasingly precarious position, since a disproportionate number were already in the lowest 10%. The economic differences between Whites and people of color as a whole continued to increase (almost all of the 1% in the highest income bracket are White), even though many Whites also faced a decline in their economic well-being (Carnoy, 1994; Oliver & Shapiro, 1995).

Organized opposition to even the surface changes resulting from the civil rights struggle and the ending of legal racial segregation began showing its teeth in the 1980s and continued to gain momentum in the 1990s. The most blatant and ugly forms of overt cultural and individual racism increased, manifested by racial hate crimes, visible hate organizations, openly racist radio talk shows, and Internet news groups promoting White supremacy.

However, opposition to anti-racist changes also occurred at the highest level of government authority. The administrations of Presidents Nixon, Reagan, and Bush played a major role in the orchestration of strategies that kept civil rights legislation from being turned into meaningful new practice. One such strategy was to appoint directors opposed to affirmative action and desegregation (some of whom were people of color) to the two federal agencies especially charged with implementing and enforcing civil rights legislation—the Commission on Civil Rights and the Equal Economic Opportunity Commission—thus virtually destroying their effectiveness.

The emergence of new arguments to justify the continuance of *covert* forms of racism and the effort to roll back legal changes played a critical role in the strategy of conservatives identified with the political Right. For the architects of the new face of racist ideology,

it is not the justice but the very meaning of racial equality which is at stake. The right, especially the new conservatives, have fought hard to institutionalize their interpretation [of racism]—focused on "equality of opportunity" and explicitly oblivious to "equality of result"—as the national "common sense." (Omi & Winant, 1986, p. 141)

The arguments of the updated face of racist ideology rest on the premise that the United States is now a racism-free, "colorblind" society. Consequently,

> the reasoning behind the opposition to any specific programs or machinery to facilitate equal employment opportunities or hiring goals, or even measures such as busing to achieve desegregated schools, was that such measures were unnecessary. . . . Not only was implementation unnecessary, it was undesirable because it conferred special favors on one group, thus discriminating against other groups. (Franklin, 1993, p. 43)

The true agenda of the new face of racism was vividly illuminated by a *Los Angeles Times* investigation that revealed that University of California (UC) Regents who voted to end affirmative action admissions for people of color also "used their influence to try to get their relatives, friends and children of business partners into UC Los Angeles, in some cases ahead of better qualified applicants who were turned away" (Frammolino, Gladstone, & Wallace, 1996, p. A1). The regents hypocritically claimed that race had nothing to do with either their vote against affirmative action or their pulling strings for themselves—even though the vast majority of students who benefited from their string-pulling just happened to be White. Therefore, by their own definition, their actions are not racist.

Another key component of the new face of racism is the removal of explicit race terms while establishing a code language that enables "White society to attack African American [and other people of color] without resorting to traditional racist language" (Stroup & Fleming, 1995, p. 35). For example, among educators terms such as *inner-city, at risk, low achieving, language deficient,* and *prone to violence* have become so linked to children of color that they begin to function as explanations of educational problems that are in reality outcomes of racist practices (Meier & Brown, 1994).

"Whites as victims" is yet another linchpin of the new racist assumptions. In a turning-things-upside-down maneuver, people of color and their White allies in the struggle against racism become the racists. A case in point is the Right's accusation that multicultural and anti-bias education is responsible for disuniting the nation, ignoring Western (White) culture and thought, and harming White children's self-esteem. These critics are responding to "actual changes in curriculum required of White students as well as students of color, and particularly changes that challenge White supremacy" (Sleeter, 1995, p. 88).

Moreover, from this perspective, any government attempts to redress the negative effects on people of color of several hundred years of legal racism is seen as victimizing Whites. As Stroup and Fleming (1995) explain: "Just as the Northern federal government had intruded in the lives of White Southerners during Reconstruction, . . . it is asserted, so now that same federal government is intruding in the lives of White people" (p. 33). Thus, many Whites blame their economic problems on government anti-poverty and other social programs "inextricably identified with inner-city Blacks" (Carnoy, 1994, p. 45). The emergence of organized, armed, and active White "militia groups" attacking government buildings and federal offices is an extreme reflection of this stance.

Ultimately, the arguments of the "new faces" of racism are designed to do what the ideology of racism has always attempted to do—justify institutional, cultural, and individual racism—but this time in relation to the changing structural dynamics that emerged from the ending of legal segregation. Indeed, while masquerading with new faces, racism and racist ideology are alive and kicking in America.

CHAPTER 2

The Individual, Racism, and Anti-Racism

[B]eloved community is formed not by the eradication of difference but by its affirmation, by each of us claiming the identities and cultural legacies that shape who we are and how we live in the world. . . . We deepen those bondings by connecting with an anti-racist struggle.

—*bell hooks,* Killing Rage

In this chapter, we discuss how racism affects us as individuals and the choices that individuals make in responding to it. We distinguish between the dynamics affecting Whites and people of color, and we explore the social-psychological transformations inherent in the process of becoming anti-racist.

Analysis of individual racism must be framed within a structural context. As Frankenberg (1993) points out, "any system of differentiation shapes those on whom it bestows privilege as well as those it oppresses. White people are 'raced,' just as men are 'gendered'" (p. 1).

An individual's structural position mediates how he or she experiences racism and reproduces racist relationships—first, through membership in either the dominant or subordinate group, and second, in particular gender, ethnic, and class groups. Therefore, while it is individuals who actually carry out the daily interactions that perpetuate or countervail against racism, the significance of their behavior must be interpreted within the framework of the social meaning of their acts.

ANTI-RACISM AND THE INDIVIDUAL

As we contended in the previous chapter, racist behavior is measured by its outcomes for people of color, rather than its intentions. Yet, if the individual's behavior is measured by its objective consequences, then where do the individual's consciousness, attitudes, and intent come into the picture? Are these subjective factors irrelevant to the perpetuation of racism? Because all individuals in a racist society are involved in its relationships, does this mean that we are all immutably caught in perpetuating it? We do not believe so, and that is why we are anti-racism educators.

While racist behavior does not exist outside the system of institutionalized racism, the system cannot exist outside of individual actions. Human beings are products of the society into which they are born, but they are also actors who bring institutional relationships to life and hence have the potential for influencing and changing these relationships. Individuals thus contribute to both the maintenance and the evolution of a racist system. In these dynamic interactions lie the mechanism for either perpetuation of racism or its transformation.

People cannot choose to remove themselves from the racist system and become "nonracist," because it is impossible not to participate in an institutionally racist system. However, they can choose to change it—to consciously seek to reduce and eventually eliminate racism, and in its place to create new institutional relationships not dependent on domination and subordination of any racial groups. Here, individual intent and attitude become critical because they influence whether a person chooses to acquiesce passively or to resist.

People of color and Whites in every generation have chosen to resist racism, as the history of the United States (and other countries) vividly demonstrates (Aptheker, 1993; Hilliard, 1995). From the colonial period, to the revolts against slavery and the fight for abolition, to the Reconstruction period, to the civil rights struggles of the 1950s and 1960s, and to the current anti-racism organizing efforts, racism "has never been without substantial challenge" (Aptheker, 1993, p. 15). Whatever reduction has occurred in the worse forms of overt racism is a result of these collective, anti-racist endeavors.

Since both institutional and personal changes are necessary, however, we face a paradox. On the one hand, since institutional relationships propagate individual racist behavior, the distribution of power and resources among racial groups must first be restructured so that our social systems no longer produce racists. On the other hand, for institutional transformation to occur, individuals must change since they ultimately either reproduce the status quo or create new institutional relationships. For individuals committed to anti-racism, unlearning the basic patterns of racist thoughts and actions must be the preparation for creating new institutional relationships, making it possible to dismantle the engine that drives racism overall.

Thus, while ultimately targeting the institutionalized system of racism, anti-racism education requires an immediate focus on the individual. Though placing the blame for racism on the institutions of our society, anti-racism education does ask individuals to become accountable. The goal is to generate development of individual consciousness and skills that enable people to be active initiators of change rather than conforming perpetuators or passive victims of social oppression.

Since all individuals who live in a racist system are enmeshed in its relationships, this means that all are responsible for its perpetuation or transformation. There are no bystanders and neutral observers: Each person is either part of the problem or part of the solution. Nevertheless, the situation is complex because, while both dominant and dominated groups play roles in keeping racism alive, the responsibility is not equally shared.

WHITE RACISM / WHITE ANTI-RACISM

Racism in the United States is a White problem. Whites established the system in the first place, control its resources and power, and also have the primary power to transform it. Moreover, simply by virtue of birth into the dominant racial group, all Whites inherit a multifaceted system that asserts that White is right and that provides benefits and privileges for them. In this sense, all Whites are racists. However, this does not mean that all Whites equally possess the power to create and implement racist practices, benefit equally from racism, have consciously chosen to participate, or even want to oppress people of color.

Many Whites are in the ambiguous position of being on the privileged side of one form of institutional oppression (i.e., racism), and on the losing side of others (i.e., classism and sexism). Class, gender, and ethnic background undercut the privileges of racism for women, working-class men, and White ethnic groups that have been on the receiving end of discrimination (e.g., Jews, Irish Americans, and Italian Americans). In fact, when the benefits of racism are weighed against the losses from other institutional forms of oppression, racism not only undercuts but is contrary to the self-interest of many Whites. By accepting the notion of White superiority, those Whites who are low on the receiving end of political and economic resources and rewards objectively collude in their own economic exploitation and weaken their chances of making alliances with people of color in ending institutional oppression. Racism often plays a primary role in dividing people with common problems—such as women, men who are among the working poor and near-poor, and persons whose cultural roots are not Western European Protestant. Overt racist groups such as the Ku Klux Klan and the American Nazi Party illustrate yet another side of how racism harms certain White groups, for hate groups target not only people of color but also White religious groups, such as Jews and Catholics.

Only a small portion of the White population, in fact, gains the full economic, political, and cultural benefits of racism. This subgroup includes Whites who are affluent, male, adult, and generally Protestant. However, most anti-racism educators and scholars, including us, agree that while this subgroup has the primary power to create and maintain racism, all Whites receive privileges and benefits, albeit on a continuum.

Robert Terry (1975), a pioneering leader in anti-racism work with Whites, suggests that there are only three options: to be a bigot, a conformist, or a "new White." A bigot is a person who openly espouses White supremacy and works to maintain and strengthen institutional relationships of White privilege and power. A conformist is a person who, although not explicitly espousing White supremacy, conforms to the status quo by accepting more subtle forms of racism and by not participating in any attempt to make change. A conformist, in other words, practices covert racism, in contrast to the bigot, who practices overt racism.

A "new White" is a person who increasingly recognizes that Whites are the problem in race, that racism is carried by White power, closed structures, and ethnocentric culture. Standing against racism and for justice requires aggressive action to redistribute power, create open resources and institutions, and affirm cultural pluralism. A new White need not be afraid to admit he or she is racist because it is true. A new White need not be afraid to live in the ambiguity of White privilege while fighting White privilege because that is real. And a new White need not be ashamed or guilty to be White because that is a given he or she cannot change. Whites with this perspective directly attempt to create institutional change; they do not see themselves as outside of the system, but choose to transform the system.

PEOPLE OF COLOR: PRO-RACISM / ANTI-RACISM

Although racism in America is historically and structurally a White problem, people of color do play a role in perpetuating the system: Racist behavior and beliefs among the White dominating population have a kind of counterpart in the behavior and beliefs of populations victimized by racism. We call those behaviors and beliefs pro-racist rather than racist because the structural dynamics are different. Pro-racism originates in racism and reflects an acquiescence to the oppressing power structure and belief system created by racism. Conversely, racism is not a reflection of pro-racism. Racists participate in the oppression of others; pro-racists participate in oppression directed against themselves.

Racism and Pro-Racism

There is a certain irony to our assertion that persons of color participate in racism (as pro-racists) because we do not agree with much of what has been written on this subject. The ongoing debate over using the word *racist* to describe the behavior of people of color is usually not about how they contribute to their own oppression, but about their hostile attitude toward Whites.

Although the overt behaviors of the racist and pro-racist may appear identical and may equally support the status quo, it is nevertheless important to remember the distinction between the two: A racist belongs to the group that controls the institutions of American society and participates in the benefits of racism, while a pro-racist belongs to the group that is harmed by the system and, in maintaining the status quo, colludes with his own oppression. Pro-racism takes two forms: in carrying out racist policies and practices against members of other groups of color, and in carrying them out against one's own group. As with White racism, the social consequence of an individual's behavior, rather than intent, is the measure of pro-racism. For example, a human development theoretician of color who explains the disproportionate poverty of people of color by their cultural patterns, values, or child-rearing techniques colludes with the dominant society in justifying and perpetuating racism as much as a White counterpart.

The distinction between racist and pro-racist also has important implications for our perspective on the term *reverse racism*. In brief, we do not subscribe to its usage in referring to either (1) prejudices against Whites by persons of color or (2) the so-called preferential treatment accorded under affirmative action or multicultural curriculum approaches. Reverse racism has no meaning within the context of systemic, institutional power where Whites as a group hold that power and use it to deny privilege to people of color. The attempts to reverse centuries of inequality through affirmative action and cultural self-determination are not attacks on Whites, per se, but on the system of racism. The goal of these strategies is not to turn the present racial order on its head but rather to achieve an anti-racist society where all individuals have access to dignity, power, self-determination, and expectation of equal outcomes for the value of their unique contributions to society.

We do not deny that people of color may exhibit prejudice toward Whites in their personal opinions or actions, but we would describe the phenomenon by terms other than *reverse racism*—again because people of color do not have the systemic power to engage in institutional racism against Whites.

The Twin Poles of Pro-Racism and Anti-Racism

As with Whites, people of color are also challenged to unlearn the racist framework of the dominant culture, and this process often represents a journey from the pole of pro-racist conformity to the pole of active anti-racism. One of the earliest scholars to analyze the complexity of consciousness among the oppressed in the United States, Du Bois (1903, 1985), described a "dual consciousness" among Blacks—one imposed by the White world, the other emanating from the history, traditions, and longings for liberation of the Black community. He further delineated the internal conflicts created by the interactions between these two essentially opposing orientations. The more individuals internalize the dominant society's views, the more they will think and act pro-racist. The more individuals' consciousness reflects identification with their own people's history, culture, and desire for liberation, the closer they will be to acting as anti-racists.

Fanon (1967a, 1967b), another pioneer in the work of understanding the psychology of oppressed people, applied his experience with colonialism to identify different modes of response that led either to participation in one's own oppression or to resistance. He describes capitulation to oppression as involving submission and assimilation into the dominant culture, internalizing the value system and ideology of the oppressor and suppressing or rejecting the cultural values of one's own group. This is the consciousness we call pro-racism. Further, Fanon describes the contrasting mode—radicalization—in which the individual rejects the oppressor's ideology and engages in attempts to develop alternatives to awaken the consciousness of his or her people and to participate in the struggle to transform society. Moreover, the individual who is radicalized sees the struggle for liberating one's own people as part of the larger struggle of others who experience oppression. This well defines our conception of anti-racism.

Based on his extensive research, William Cross (1991) describes polar ends of a sequence of identity transformation among African Americans. In a manner that supports our conception of pro-racism and anti-racism consciousness, he describes two world views: One is dominated by Euro-American determinants, negation of Blacks and Blackness, and belief that Blacks and not the system are to blame for their own problems. This first group tends to be anti-Black and pro-White. In the other world view, African American individuals acknowledge Blacks as their primary reference group while maintaining a pluralistic nonracist perspective toward others, blaming the system rather than Blacks for racism and engaging in social activism with Blacks and other groups victimized by racism. Individuals in this second group tend to hold positive but not uncritical attitudes toward Blacks and critical but not negative attitudes toward Whites.

Antonia Darder's (1991) discussion of the process of biculturalism offers another valuable perspective on the dimensions of pro- or anti-racist consciousness. Because her work encompasses the experience of Latinos in U.S. society, it adds another dimension to the discourse. She argues that bicultural responses are best understood "in terms of an axis relationship between culture and power that, on one hand, moves between the dominant and subordinate cultures and, on the other hand, moves between the forces of dominance and resistance" (p. 54). Darder further identifies four major response patterns: alienation, dualism, separation, and negotiation. Her definition of *alienation* shares key points with our notion of pro-racism: behaviors "that suggest an internalized identification with the dominant culture and a rejection of the primary culture" (p. 55). Examples include "refusal to speak Spanish, belief in the inferiority of the primary culture, and denial of the existence of racism" (p. 55). Similarly, the definition of "cultural negotiation" resonates with our concept of anti-racism: reflecting "attempts to mediate, reconcile, and integrate the reality of lived experiences in an effort to retain the primary cultural identity and orientation while functioning toward social transformation within the society at large" (p. 56).

THE JOURNEY TO ANTI-RACIST IDENTITY

Establishment of a clear, affirming group identity and recognition of the necessity of collective action for self-determination and against racism are the hallmarks of an adult pro-liberation perspective for people of color. White anti-racism requires parallel elements: new identity as a White, a critique of racism and the institutions of White society, and a recognition of the necessity for collective action. In essence, all must undo the profound impact of the ideology of racism on their self-concepts and social perspectives. However, the process of change differs, reflecting the distinctions we have been making between people of color and Whites.

Becoming anti-racist involves a series of phases or stages that transform the individuals making the journey. We have observed the transformations in the growth of adult participants in our anti-racism course, and the observations have been validated by recent research (Cross, 1991; Darder, 1991; Helms, 1990; Tatum, 1992). The researchers have based their findings on interviews with adults reflecting various perspectives on their racial identity, observations of students' responses in classes addressing racism, and therapeutic sessions where individuals have explored personal and group identity issues. We recommend reading their important work directly. Here, we provide a summary of the key steps on the journey to anti-racist identity: Each describes an individual's frame of reference at any given time, as well as a particular point in the change cycle.

Although compelling evidence supports the idea of transformational phases, these are neither inevitable, static, nor achieved for all time. Life circumstances precipitate and support change—toward or away from anti-racism consciousness and behavior. For example, Helms (1990) states that "Whites . . . can choose environments that permit them to remain fixated at a particular stage of racial consciousness" and "each stage can culminate in either a positive or negative resolution" (p. 155). Cross (1991) suggests that each stage in his model characterizes an identity that works for some African Americans, with movement to the next stage requiring precipitating life factors. Darder (1991) also points out that individuals may utilize the four bicultural response patterns she describes at various points in their life, depending on the demands of the societal contexts in which they are at that moment. Finally, even when an individual reaches the culminating phase of anti-racist identity, life brings continuing contradictions that demand resolution and further growth.

Developmental Progression of People of Color

Du Bois (1903) and Fanon (1967a, 1967b) laid the foundation for more recent study of the stages Black people traverse in their search for a new Black identity. William Cross's (1991) model is currently the most developed and influential. Although this model is based on the African American experience, others are constructing identity development models for European Americans and Asian Americans (Hardiman, 1979; Kim, 1981). Cross (1991) characterizes his work as "a model that explains how assimilated Black adults, as well as deracinated, deculturalized or miseducated Black adults are transformed by a series of circumstances and events into persons who are more Black or Afrocentrically aligned" (p. 190). He specifies five stages in this *resocializing experience* he calls the development of *nigrescence*, "the process of becoming Black" (p. 147): (1) Pre-encounter, (2) Encounter, (3) Immersion/Emersion, (4) Internalization, and (5) Internalization-Commitment.

The Pre-encounter stage finds the individual accepting the dominant society's ideology, desiring to assimilate into and be accepted by White society, actively or passively distancing himself or herself from other Blacks, using victim-blaming explanations, and bashing Black leaders, the Black family, and Black culture. Of significance to our earlier discussion of the new faces of racism (see Chapter 1), Cross observes that White oppression, miseducation, and the success of a few exceptional Blacks have been the main factors fueling the social production of Pre-encounter attitudes.

Movement into the Encounter stage comes when a shocking personal or social event or a series of small, eye-opening episodes temporarily dislodge the individual from his or her Pre-encounter identity. "The encounter must work around, slip through, or even shatter the relevance of the person's current identity and world view, and at the same time provide some hint of the direction in which to point the person to be resocialized or transformed" (Cross, 1991, p. 199). During this time, "each individual ponders very personal questions" and will most likely experience strong emotions, including guilt and anger, that become energizing factors for change (pp. 199–201).

Immersion/Emersion, the third stage, "depicts the intense period of transition when the convert is attempting to destroy the old identity and at the same time experiment with and move toward the new identity" (Cross, 1991, p. 159). This is a time characterized by a powerful desire to learn about and glorify the African heritage, a tendency to deify Black culture and Black people, anxiety about whether one is becoming the "right kind" of Black, applying a Blacker-than-thou syndrome, and demonizing and rejecting White people and White culture. This is the most difficult time in the progression of change. As it comes to an end, the individual begins to feel in greater control of himself or herself.

The fourth and fifth stages, Internalization and Internalization-Commitment, are similar to our concept of an anti-racist identity in people of color. Internalization signals the resolution of conflict between the old and new world views. "If Encounter and Immersion-Emersion usher in cognitive dissonance and an accompanying roller-coaster emotionality, then the Internalization stage marks the point of dissonance resolution. . . . The person feels calmer, more relaxed, more at ease with self" (Cross, 1991, p. 210). Confidence in one's personal standards of Blackness, controlled anger toward racist institutions, dedicated long-term commitment, a sense of destiny, Black pride, self-love, and a sense of Black communalism are attributes of this stage. Anti-White feelings decline to the point where friendships with White associates can be renegotiated, and a person's strong sense of group identity also "becomes the point of departure for discovering the universe of ideas, cultures and experiences beyond Blackness" (Cross, Parham, & Helms, 1991, p. 330). Finally, in the fifth stage, the individual person is a social activist, devoting "an extended period, if not a lifetime, to finding ways to translate their personal sense of Blackness into a plan of action or a general sense of commitment" (Cross, 1991, p. 220). However, Cross declares that

> current theory suggests that there are few differences between the psychology of Blacks at the fourth and fifth stages of nigrescence other than the important factor of sustained interest and commitment. . . . Consequently, . . . a more differentiated look at Internalization-Commitment awaits the results of future research. (p. 220)

Finally, we want to reiterate Tatum's (1992) point that "though the process of racial identity development has been represented here in linear form, in fact it is probably more accurate to think of it in a spiral form" (p. 12). Moreover, a person may "revisit an earlier stage as the result of new encounter experiences, though the later experience of the stage may be different from the original experience" (p. 12).

Whites' Developmental Progression

Helms's work (1984, 1990) was the first published comprehensive examination of how Whites develop attitudes about being White. As she pointed out, in the psychological literature "personal identity development is ignored in favor of inferring social adaptability from racial attitudes toward other groups" (1984, p. 155). This situation reflects most Whites' denial that their racial identify has any significance, seeing themselves only as individuals and, consequently, not responsible for perpetuating a racist system.

Helms's model of White racial identity development specifies five stages: Contact, Disintegration, Reintegration, Pseudo-Independence, and Autonomy. The Contact stage begins when a White individual becomes aware that Black people exist. Defining characteristics at this point include naiveté, fear, and lack of knowledge about people of color; unawareness of oneself as a racial being; tendency either to ignore differences or regard them as unimportant (colorblindness); and lack of awareness of cultural and institutional racism. In our definition of racist behavior, these attributes enable a White to participate in covert racism even without conscious intent. Whites whose lives limit their interactions with people of color and their awareness of racial issues may remain at this stage indefinitely

(Tatum, 1992). However, confusing experiences with people of color and/or negative reactions of Whites to interracial associations, as well as exposure to new information about racism, may usher in the next stage, Disintegration. Now, as the individual becomes aware that racism exists and is forced to acknowledge his or her Whiteness and the part he or she plays in perpetuating racism, feelings of guilt and depression arise. Helms postulates three ways of resolving these uncomfortable feelings: (1) attempt to overidentify with people of color, (2) become paternalistic, (3) retreat into the predictability of White culture.

Either through rejection by people of color as a result of choosing solution 1 or 2, or societal pressure to conform to the status quo of race relationships, the individual is pushed into stage three—Reintegration. Two reactions may occur at this time. One is a withdrawal into Whiteness, and the other is further examination that leads to anti-racism. For those who withdraw into conformity with racist norms, feelings generated in the Disintegration stage "may be redirected in the form of fear and anger toward people of color (particularly Blacks), who are now blamed as the source of discomfort" (Tatum, 1992, p. 15). According to Helms (1990), Whites can easily become stuck at this stage of development. However, if there is support for continued self-examination and the individual begins to face the social/political implication of being White in a racist society, then the alternative becomes possible—movement into the fourth stage.

Helms's fourth and fifth stages correspond to our concept of anti-racist White identity. During Pseudo-Independence, individuals make a conscious effort to disconnect themselves from racist behavior and covert acquiescence to White power, seeking instead to replace conformity to racism with a world view that affirms the value of all people and cultures and, further, seeks to share power and resources. Those who reach Autonomy, the fifth stage, have learned how to be autonomous Whites, functioning as self-actualized individuals and joining with people of color and other exploited groups to change racist systems.

CONCLUSIONS

As you will see in the following chapters, we also discovered that both White students and students of color participated in a transformational process with identifiable phases in their journeys from racist and pro-racist to anti-racist consciousness. The differences between racial groups reflected what the literature we have cited would predict regarding the transformations actually observed in our anti-racism course. In general, we found that students of color moved—

1. From rejection of and alienation from their own racial/cultural identity to reclamation and affirmation of who they are (with new identities based on their own definitions of themselves, not those of the dominant society)

2. From submission to the dominant society's explanation of racism, including self-blame, to a frame of reference that located responsibility for the creation and evolution of racism to the institutions of the dominant society
3. From collusion with their own oppression through direct acts or through passivity to active engagement in individual and collective anti-racist acts

White students moved—

1. From ethnocentric, unthinking acceptance of their racial group to development of a White identity that reconnected with and sought to keep that which is good and abolish that which is bad in a European American culture
2. From individualistic or victim-blaming explanations of racism to a critique of institutional structures and acceptance of responsibility of racism as a White problem
3. From participation in racism through acts of commission or omission to active anti-racist activity, individually and with others

While creation of a new identity requires people of color to first break away from the dominant culture, reconnect with their own group, and then find ways to reestablish connections with the dominant culture based on a new sense of identity, Whites must first distance themselves from their own group, determine what they want to keep and discard, and then establish a new identity that enables them to maintain a dual relationship to their group—reconnecting, on one hand, and challenging its roles and racism on the other. Similarly, establishing a new perspective about the nature of racism requires Whites to comprehend the dynamics of being part of the oppressor group, while people of color must comprehend the dynamics of being part of the oppressed group. Last, commitment to anti-racism activity challenges Whites to break the "gentleman's agreement" of silence among Whites, to take a stand against members of their own group, and to face the partial loss of White privilege. Anti-racist activity challenges people of color to find the courage to confront their oppressors, to survive the more severe penalties historically meted out to those who refuse to submit, and to create alliances with other people of color and groups hurt by institutional oppression.

Having established in Chapters 1 and 2 the conceptual context from which our course derives, we now turn to the main entree: what it looks like to implement pedagogy that challenges and guides students, and supports their journeys to anti-racism.

PART II

Racism and Human Development: The Class

This part of the book describes the chronological progression of a semester course on anti-racism education. The division into four chapters reflects the four phases—conflict, disequilibrium, transformation, and activism—through which students go to achieve the anti-racist consciousness and behavior that are the goals of the course. To illuminate the interactional nature of the teaching-learning process, each chapter discusses the class from three perspectives:

- The teaching challenges of the particular phase of development
- The activities and teaching strategies for each class session
- Student responses (illustrated by material from their journals) and our analysis of student growth

Our Racism and Human Development course consists of a 3-hour weekly class, conducted for 15 weeks, with about 20–25 students. It is designed for upper-division baccalaureate and master's-level students specializing in early childhood education and related human service professions. The course is co-taught by an interracial team; methods are varied and include experiential activities, films and videotapes, large- and small-group discussions, and lectures. The students have extensive reading assignments, keep journals of their reflections on the class, and undertake projects in and outside of class. The curriculum content and sequence reflect our understanding of the steps that enable students to move successfully toward anti-racist consciousness and behavior.

The tone of the narrative in these chapters is intended to engage the reader personally in the experience. Therefore much of the writing is in the first person, and students are identified by name (though all names are fictional) and at times with some background information. Although we have quoted only a relatively small portion of the students' comments, they represent the facts and feelings reflected in the journals of many in the class.

To help you maintain a concept of the whole while delving into the detail of the specific parts of this multidimensional experience, we are providing the following overview of the course:

Week 1 **Setting the Scene**

An introduction to the course and each other

Activity 1: Describing the Course
Activity 2: Introductions of Students

Assignment for completion by next week: 2–3 page racial and
ethnic identity paper

Week 2 **Exploring Personal Dimensions**

*Development of students' awareness of their own ethnic iden-
tity in the context of a racist society*

Activity 1: Small-Group Discussions of Racial and Ethnic Iden-
tity Paper
Activity 2: Large-Group Discussions of Racial and Ethnic
Identity

Week 3 **Uncovering Attitudes and Experiences**

*An exploration of personal knowledge, attitudes, and experi-
ence with interracial encounters, with preparation for connecting experience to societal institutions*

Activity 1: Cultural Questionnaire and Discussion
Activity 2: Small-Group Discussion of "Hard Moments"

Reading assignment: *Killers of the Dream* (Smith, 1962)

Week 4 **Institutional Racism**

*Concepts of individual, institutional, overt, and covert racism;
connection of personal experience to systemic racism; exploration of the relationship between individual and institutional racism*

Activity 1: The Drawbridge Exercise
Activity 2: Definitions and Forms of Racism

Reading assignment: *Roots of Racism & Patterns of Racism* (Institute of Race Relations, 1982)

Week 5 **Action Projects and Victim-Blaming**

*Preparation for student project in anti-racist action and explo-
ration of victim-blaming as a racist rationalization*

Activity 1: Action Project (assignment and preparation)
Activity 2: Victim-Blaming Lecture

Reading assignment: *Blaming the Victim* (Ryan, 1976)

Week 6 Taking Stock

A coming to grips with personal tensions and a deepening understanding of how to direct these feelings toward the development of anti-racist consciousness and behavior

Activity 1: Children and Racism: An examination of children's books
Activity 2: How Are You Feeling So Far? Each student shares feelings

Reading assignment in class: *Children, Race and Racism: How Race Awareness Develops* (Derman-Sparks, Higa, & Sparks, 1980)
Reading after the session: Talking about race, learning about racism: *The Application of Racial Identity Development Theory in the Classroom* (Tatum, 1992)

Week 7 Sexism, Classism, and Racism

Examination of gender, class, and other factors in the context of racism

Activity 1: Class Identity Groups
Activity 2: *Salt of the Earth* (film)

Reading assignments: *This Bridge Called My Back* (Moraga & Anyaldua, 1981) or *Women, Race & Class* (Davis, 1983) or *Race, Class, and Gender* (Anderson & Collins, 1995)

Week 8 Moving into Action

Further development of action projects and a deeper exploration of cultural identity

Activity 1: Action Project Support Groups
Activity 2: Exploring Cultural Identity

Reading assignment: A novel or autobiography about an ethnic group in the United States that is different from one's own and whose author is from the ethnic group that is the subject of the book (this assignment continues through week 9)

Week 9   **Culture, Values, and Behavior**

> *An examination of culture (as distinguished from race), including an increased understanding of cultural differences and the development of strategies for working with culturally diverse people*

Activity 1: The "BaFá BaFá": A copyrighted game (*BaFá BaFá*, 1977)
Activity 2: An Anthropologic Framework for Thinking About Culture

Reading assignment: See Week 8

Week 10   **Culture, Values, and Behavior Continued**

> *Examination of both cultural groups in the United States and the imposition of European American values on those outside the United States*

Activity 1: Learning About Cultures
Activity 2: Examining the Impact of Racism on Cultures Beyond the United States

Reading assignment: *The Colonizer and the Colonized* (Memmi, 1965)

Week 11   **Cultural Diversity, Racism, and Education**

> *Deepening understanding of "culturally relevant" approaches to education and the barriers to their implementation*

Activity 1: Culture and Learning Styles
Activity 2: A Critique of IQ

Reading assignments: *The Mismeasure of Man* (Gould, 1981) or *Even the Rat Was White: A Historical View of Psychology* (Guthrie, 1976); also *The Dreamkeepers* (Ladson-Billings, 1994) or *Meeting the Challenge of Linguistic and Cultural Diversity in Early Childhood Education* (Garcia & McLaughlin, 1995) or *Diversity in the Classroom: New Approaches to the Education of Young Children* (Kendall, 1995)

Week 12   **Alternative Adult Educational Models**

> *An exploration of models that can empower people who have been disenfranchised by institutionalized racism and other forms of oppression*

Small and large group discussions explore the use of Freire's educational ideas

Reading assignment: *Pedagogy of the Oppressed* (Freire, 1970)

Week 13 Activist Role Models for Anti-Racism

Learning through role models who are known for their exemplary anti-racism work

Guest speakers are introduced and have a chance to describe their anti-racism work; students have an opportunity to ask questions and meet the guests one-on-one

Week 14 Evaluating Action Projects

An opportunity to present one's own project and to learn about all of the strategies and experiences in the entire class

Activity 1: Final Reports (support groups)
Activity 2: Report to Class of Action Projects' Strategies and Challenges

Students submit papers about action projects to the instructors

Week 15 Where Do We Go from Here?

An opportunity to review strategies and resources that will continue to be available to the students, a reflection on the meaning of the course, and a time to make a personal commitment to anti-racist behavior and action

Activity 1: Reviewing Strategies and Resources
Activity 2: What Has the Course Meant to You?

CHAPTER 3

The First Phase: Beginning
Explorations of Racism

People have asked us on several occasions why students take an anti-racism course. Reasons vary. Most Whites think it will be about the cultures of people of color; most people of color take it because inclusion of racism in a course description piques their curiosity and because one of the instructors is a person of color. Some take it because the course is required in their program. No one anticipates what actually happens to them. As one student declared in her last session, "I thought I was taking a class; it turned out to be a life event."

TEACHING CHALLENGES

The frames of reference students bring to the class is our starting point. The initial pedagogical task is to awaken them to the inadequacies, contradictions, and tensions in their adaptations to racism. These must be uncovered, named, and disrupted for further growth to occur. In other words, the first task is to prepare students for learning. Understanding the multiple elements and dynamics of the consciousness that students bring with them makes the successful achievement of this first task much more likely.

It is important to remember that students have, for the most part, invested considerable emotional energy in maintaining and protecting their adaptations and accommodations to racism. Their self-identity is intimately tied to their solutions. Even if unresolved questions, confusion, and tensions continue to plague them, they have learned to live and work within the context of their adaptations, and will not, in most cases, willingly give up their package of ideas and behaviors without a struggle. Consequently, students exhibit various kinds of resistance: White students may focus on students of color instead of on their own issues, and vice versa, or students may intellectualize by talking about the human condition in general, insist that the course is irrelevant to their needs, or simply keep silent. Our task is to create an environment where all students can uncover and begin examining previously unexamined attitudes, beliefs, and feelings; explore the implications for identity and role in systemic racism; and discover the contradictions and tensions in their understanding of and stance toward racism.

During this time, students are very sensitive to nuances of teacher behavior. Consequently, our attitudes and behavior must consistently reflect respect and support for all students; none are negatively judged because they reveal racist or pro-racist attitudes or ignorance—which they can be counted on to do. We must also convey our conviction that everyone must struggle with the effects of being raised in a racist society, including us, and that we can change if we so choose.

However, at the same time, it is also necessary to gradually increase gentle, respectful, but incisive probing that helps students more deeply uncover their confusion, tensions, and misinformation. While we do not expect them to be completely frank or self-disclosing all at once, we are sometimes amazed at the amount of information students offer about themselves very early in the course—giving people permission to talk about a topic previously forbidden unleashes a wave of confidences. Learning to be anti-racist is like eating an artichoke one layer at a time, from the outer, less meaty leaves to the heart of the matter. The kinds of questions we ask are guided by this metaphor. In weeks one and two, we want them to deal with some of the outer layers of the artichoke.

The start of the class generates conflicting feelings in us. On the one hand, there is a sense of excitement and anticipation regarding the journey we are asking students to take with us. It is always a marvel to watch students grow as they come to a deeper understanding of their lives, reclaim their full humanity, and gain the strength to act. On the other hand, we also experience stage fright. Will we have the energy, the patience, the discipline not only to launch the journey, but to guide each student skillfully as far as each can go?

The degree of self-control required in the first weeks of the course is taxing. Students' prejudiced comments and revelations of hurtful experiences can leave us feeling dirty, bruised, hurt, and angry. Yet our responsibility is to remain neutral in these early weeks, to make it possible for students to uncover for themselves the very attitudes, ideas, and feelings they must face and work to change. It is also important to listen very carefully and to keep quiet unless we need to support a student through a question or to redirect a student who digresses from focusing on herself or himself. To maintain self-control without too great expense, we make sure that we take time after each class to debrief our feelings in addition to talking about our sense of each student's beginning place. We also find it helpful to remind each other why we are teaching the course in the first place. And we hope that both of us will not feel too overwhelmed at the same moment!

ACTIVITIES

Achieving insights into the social meaning of one's personal experiences is key to developing anti-racist consciousness. Weeks one and two involve setting the scene, introducing concepts and examples, exploring personal dimensions of racism, and gaining a better understanding of identity. These class sessions encourage students to engage in both introspection and reflection—to identify the realities in their lives, uncover buried and obscured memories, and gain a new perspective on the meaning of race, ethnicity, and racism in their lives. The pace is slow and calculated, intended mainly to make these experiences accessible to students and for us to mark the place from which change can be measured.

Week 1: Setting the Scene

This session introduces students to the course, to us, and to each other. Chairs are arranged in a circle so that everyone can see each other.

Activity 1: Describing the Course. We begin by making a statement about the purposes and focus of the course, emphasizing five basic premises:

1. The primary topic of the class is racism—how it operates to affect us all; how we are socialized to think, feel, and act in racist and pro-racist ways; and, finally, how to confront, resist, and change it.
2. Although we all need to understand the impact of a racist society on us as individuals and on our professional work, there are some distinct and important differences between the experiences of Whites and those of people of color.
3. People can transform unwanted racist and pro-racist attitudes and behavior. We know this because we have seen it happen in previous courses.
4. Learning to be anti-racist is difficult, anxiety-producing, and painful, requiring learning and change at many levels. We will create a nurturing environment for this growth and will be available for support through the process of change.
5. Becoming anti-racist is worth the struggle because the personal results are liberating growth and an increased sense of self-esteem.

In addition, we share a little about our own growth in becoming anti-racist, describing some of our own struggles, pain, and fears, and, ultimately, our new and stronger sense of ourselves. Moreover, we emphasize that we are still participants in the learning process; each time we teach this class, we gain further insights into ourselves, the dynamics of racism, and the process of becoming anti-racist.

Finally, we provide an overview of the course and expectations for participation by reviewing the syllabus and course requirements. Regular attendance is essential, along with weekly reading assignments (some required and some self-selected), journal writing, and an "action project." We reassure students that we will assist all of them to individualize their work in light of their own needs and interests, helping them to find manageable and useful activities. Defining these parameters is basic to a good beginning because most students initially expect that a class on racism would be a study of people of color.

Activity 2: Introductions of Students. One at a time, students are asked to introduce themselves by describing—

1. Their ethnic and class background and family structure
2. The racial composition of their neighborhood and school while they were growing up
3. Family attitudes about their own ethnicity and the ethnicity of others
4. Concrete experiences with people different from themselves
5. Concrete experiences with racial prejudice
6. Civil rights or anti-racist activities in which they have participated

We introduce ourselves first to provide examples of what students should talk about, to model disclosing embarrassing or uncomfortable information, and to decrease the distance between ourselves and students.

Through these introductions, students weave a rich tapestry depicting the diversity of real-life experiences with racism. The enormous detail lays the basis for future reflection and examination.

Our teaching strategies seek to ensure that the introductions will fulfill their intended purposes. We list these strategies below:

1. *Requiring everyone to take a turn.* To keep the flow of students talking, we encourage listening—no questions, comments, or other interruptions.
2. *Being nonjudgmental.* As students share childhood memories, some blatant racism is expressed. No comments or, if necessary, neutral ones are appropriate. We avoid disapproving facial expressions or body language. We convey acceptance and support to all students regardless of what they might say, through eye contact as they speak, encouragement when they have difficulty, and when the comments are particularly honest or painful, through positive feedback acknowledging their efforts. At the same time, we note attitudes and beliefs we think will require further work.
3. *Focusing students on their own stories.* Stories sometimes wander away from responses to the specific questions we pose, or turn into abstractions. We bring students back to the subject by a direct question that focuses them on concrete situations in their own lives.
4. *Deflecting premature confrontations.* Questions such as "Don't you think we're really all alike?" or "Can I ask White people how they got to feel this way?" have the potential to divert attention from individual experiences and to provoke confrontation too early in the class. We bring the focus back to personal experience and indicate that we will talk about those subjects later in the course.

5. *Bringing closure*. After the last introduction is completed, several brief comments from the instructors serve to acknowledge that the intent of the exercise has been achieved. We thank students for their openness, point out how much their stories show that racism affects everyone's life, and explain that they will have greater clarity about the meaning of their experiences as the course progresses.
6. *Keeping notes*. Specific incidents related by students are sometimes useful for discussing issues later in the semester, and we make note of these for future planning.

Week 2: Exploring Personal Dimensions

The next session continues to open up students' awareness of the dynamics of their ethnic identity and the ways their personal lives connect to the dynamics of a racist society. The sharpening process requires articulation of their experiences and feelings, making these available to conscious analysis and critique. It also requires recognizing that their experiences have both personal and social meaning.

Activity 1: Small-Group Discussions of Racial and Ethnic Identity Paper. We give the following assignment to the students at the end of the first week's class:

> Write a 2- to 3-page paper describing memories of learning about race and racism. Focus on childhood experiences affecting what you know and feel about your own racial and ethnic identity and what you know and feel about groups different from your own.

In groups of four or five, students use the following questions as a framework for sharing the experiences and feelings they described in their ethnic identity papers. Each person has 10 to 15 minutes. (One student keeps notes to be used later in a full-group discussion.)

1. Are you clear about your ethnic/racial identity? If yes, why do you think you are clear? If no, why do you think you are not clear?
2. Who/what were the most significant influences in the establishment of your ethnic/racial identity?
3. What feelings did you experience when writing the paper? How do these feelings compare or contrast with those of others in the group?
4. What patterns, themes, or issues emerged from the group discussion regarding your experiences?

We ask students not to criticize or confront each other but to be supportive and ask questions only for clarification. Although pointing out racism in each other will be useful later in the semester when stronger relationships exist, we explain that judgmental remarks at this time stop people from exposing true feelings and beliefs.

During the small-group discussion, we circulate, listen, and facilitate the groups as necessary. Typically the discussions are vigorous and animated. Peripheral monitoring is usually sufficient, and instructors need to interrupt only when groups go way off the subject. Refocusing the group on one of the questions or probing for more discussion about an incident someone has already shared gets them back on track.

Activity 2: Large-Group Discussions of Racial and Ethnic Identity. After these conversations conclude, we lead a whole-class discussion of the patterns, issues, and feelings that emerged in the small groups. Our purpose is to help students discover the social meaning of their individual experiences through identifying and reflecting on these themes. We highlight the themes that emerge from the groups, and, if the following issues have not arisen, ask:

- What discomfort about being White have people felt?
- What double messages were heard from parents?
- How does it feel to have a strong ethnic identity? To be without one?
- What does it mean to be "colorblind?"
- What are the unresolved conflicts about race and racism?

STUDENT RESPONSES

Students disclose a surprising amount of personal information during these first two sessions, even though most class members have not met before. Students use the permission and safety of the setting to talk openly about racial issues. When one classmate speaks, the others discover buried memories of past events. Many students relate afterward that this was the first time they had ever shared information about their racial identity. Some are exhilarated by the experience; some are uncomfortable. Some feel anxious about how they will sound when it is their turn to speak. In one way or another, talking about themselves opens up important issues and arouses emotion.

Initial Perceptions

About three-quarters of the White students not only perceive themselves as nonracist, but also expect others to. One astute participant asked after the end of her first class:

Were we all trying to impress each other with how nonracist we are? I guess because it was my concern, I focused on it. All I kept hearing was talk such as "Well, I was taught everyone was the same" or "It didn't matter to me what he or she was." I thought it sounded like we were the good White guys.

The uncomfortable discovery that the course seeks to help them uncover their racism leads to White students' wanting to affirm a rationale for their self-perceptions. Five patterns are discernible:

1. *"I'm not a racist."* According to their definitions, racists espouse White superiority, bigoted attitudes, racial separation, and overt acts of discrimination. Their claim to belief in the equality of all humans, equal opportunity, and the insignificance of racial differences makes them, by definition, not racist.
2. *"For me, anti-racism training is irrelevant."* Judy exemplifies this position:

   I feel that I do not need this class. I'm only taking it because I have to have a multicultural course for my degree. Frankly, there is no problem for me. I have a good friend who is Black and we get along fine. We are very much alike. I don't really even notice which color my children at work are—White, Black, green, or purple. They are children and I treat them all the same. Frankly, I don't see how the topic of this class could have any relevance for my teaching.

3. *"Racism isn't my responsibility."* Students taking this position argue that they personally did not cause racism to exist. "Should the sons and daughters bear the burden for their fathers' sins?"
4. *"Talking about racism creates unpleasantness."* Martha speaks for this position:

   Talking about racism makes me uneasy, upset, and frustrated. I do not want to subject myself to such miserable feelings. Besides, I think talking about racism is divisive. We should think positive and learn about the good things in different groups. . . . I don't watch movies like *Holocaust* or read books like *Roots* because they show too much about racial hatred that would better be forgotten.

5. *"Racism isn't a priority."* Students who fit this pattern declare, like Frank,

   Although I probably need much more background about it, I am much more interested in other prejudices like handicappism and prejudice against fat people. I am also interested in looking at sexism and ageism.

Others claim that a course about racism has no direct meaning for them because they are working with Whites or plan to work only with them.

The remaining one-quarter of the White students, either initially or by the end of the first session, acknowledge a need to learn more about racism:

> As I started to think about the class, I realized I knew nothing about my own or anyone else's racism. I did not even know my feelings toward racism. It is an issue I simply have never thought about.

Some are open and nondefensive, welcoming the opportunity to explore issues usually considered taboo:

> What an interesting, very different type of class. I feel comfortable here. A real surprise. I am free to feel what I am feeling and to express those feelings. I know that I'm afraid of certain racial groups, and I don't like those feelings. They bind me up inside, and I find myself making judgments based on fear. This class is really the first time I've been able to express these fears without being ridiculed or having the situation joked about. I'm afraid we of the White middle-class are in for a few hard times, but I'm really looking forward to the learning I will be able to do.

Others are "apprehensive":

> I left the class with a lot of mixed feelings. To begin with, I did not know what to expect. Racists to me were members of the KKK, not people like me. I found myself getting very nervous and apprehensive. I really didn't think I needed to deal with racism, but by the end of the first night I knew I did.

Students of color also initially view themselves as nonracist. But in contrast with Whites, they do not feel a need to affirm such self-perception or to elaborate a rationale for their thinking. By virtue of their experiences as the "victims of racism," their status is a "given," not requiring them to defend their assumptions or examine themselves. They simply do not consider themselves in need of anti-racism training. Instead, the initial reactions reflected in their journal entries are mainly judgments about Whites or reflections about how angry they feel talking with Whites about racism.

1. *"I'll wait and see."* Quiet curiosity characterizes students like Boyce, who wrote, "I kept my ears opened and my mouth shut. I wanted to see from what perspective everyone else was coming."
2. *"These Whites are a trip."* Some comments are sympathetic:

> I was aware of the sincere honesty on the part of students. I was not fully aware of the way Whites really felt and how confused they are

and how they don't understand why they feel as they do about certain issues.

Yet, others who feel that "Whites are a trip" are critical and judgmental:

> These Whites really can't understand. Every time the subject of Blacks being oppressed and discriminated against comes up, they want to minimize it by finding another group of people who are being treated similarly.

3. *"Do I have to get angry and drained about this all over again?"* Barbara exemplifies this response:

> It was draining to listen, but everything was okay until hearing a student use the expression "Black list." Then it began to get on my nerves. During break, I suggested she not use the term and was told I was too sensitive. That just added to my drained feelings and my weakening trust.

4. *"I'm not sure I really want to do this in public."* For example, Anita declares: "I'm not sure that this class is the forum I personally care to use to make a declaration to the world about my ethnicity."

Although distancing is the predominant initial response, some students do perceive a need, even as victims of racism, to articulate uneasiness about racial issues in their own lives. Bernice admits,

> I realized, though, that during my introduction I hadn't shared anything on my ethnic background or treatment I received because I was Black. I felt bad and wondered what my teachers and classmates thought. . . . I do know that I'm going to work on whatever it is that made me feel the way I did (scared) about sharing ethnic information when at other times I have had no problem.

What do these first responses reveal about the consciousness of our students as they begin their journey toward anti-racism? The majority of students of color feel that the topic requires them to react to the racism of Whites but not to make any changes in their own consciousness or behavior. They were reluctant to admit or even consider their feelings about the damage racism has caused in their personal lives, yet they revealed the need to give vent to profound anger. The White students, for the most part, insist on their nonracism and refuse to accept any responsibility for racism. They think the class will be about people of color. Yet a few show an openness to facing what racism means.

As students, both White and of color, digest the information from the first class and begin to write ethnic identity papers, more feelings are stirred and more thoughts revealed. Two primary themes characterize the data from their exploration of childhood racial and ethnic memories: (1) double messages from home, or between home and society, and (2) unresolved latent conflicts about race and racism, which began very early in life and which remain, to date, unresolved.

White Students

Most of our White students grew up in all-White environments where people of color exist on the fringes. Many have had no sustained personal interaction with a person of color until adolescence or young adulthood. Ann recalls:

> The world I grew up in was basically White. There were religious or ethnic differences, but basically we were all the same. Our dads were at work and our moms stayed home and did Girl Scouts and PTA. I knew that Blacks lived in our town, but they were in another part that seemed like another world and to which I never went.

For some, these early experience led them to believe that everyone was White. Judy comments, "As a young child, I wasn't aware that people were different. Our maid was Black, but I always thought she fell into an oil barrel; that's what she told me, and I believed it." Similarly, Barbara describes how she remembers handling racial differences: "Even though other people might have different skin colors or live in different cultures with piñatas or kimonos, I felt that everyone was still White. They were just playing dress-up."

These White-centered cocoons, however, did not preclude learning about people of color. Most Whites remember specific instances in which they were taught, in ways that were sometimes obvious, sometimes subtle, that nonwhites were to be kept at a distance. Ruth's education from her parents was direct and obvious. She recalls:

> Growing up in a small town in Idaho, the first (earliest) thing I remember is my Black doll, a favorite one. My mother called her "Nigger Baby" or "Pickaninny." She probably still uses those terms. My mother also told us stories that portrayed Blacks as stupid, superstitious, and humorous. My older brothers told similar stories about "Pedro" and "Jose." However, my father did not disguise the messages in funny stories. His was a bitter hatred of any different ethnic or racial group. His grandfather had lost his land and his slaves as a result of the Civil War and the resentment of this experience had been passed down in the family. In sum, I was taught that "those folk" were strange, different, and inferior and people like us were normal, right, and superior.

In contrast, Frank describes the indirect negative messages he learned from parents who supposedly wanted to teach him to regard all races of people as equal:

> I didn't know or play with anyone at school of nonwhite background because there weren't any. My parents had only Anglo friends. I remember one discussion between them about inviting a Black couple over and what the neighbors were going to say. I remember wondering about what Blacks must really be like if my parents were so concerned about this. However, they gave me strict orders never to discriminate or to use racial slurs. In fact, I can remember having the feeling that being colorblind was very important to my parents. I grew into a pattern of pretending I didn't notice color, but also remember believing that I had to go out of my way to be nice to a Black person—more even than I would have been to an equivalent Anglo.

Martha reported similar experiences. Although her family valued her maternal grandfather's participation in the Underground Railroad, her contact with people of color was very limited. She writes:

> I don't recall having any day-to-day experiences that touched my life until we had a cleaning lady come in once a week. In our trips to take her home, I can remember the feeling that I had of wonderment and distaste because of the way people lived there. Everything was different. I don't recall feeling afraid; just depressed and uneasy. I find that even though I grew up wanting to love everyone, I have a locked-in fear and inability to accept differences. Even though in adulthood I have encountered many people of different races and classes, I have not overcome my uneasiness in this area.

The childhoods of many White students are characterized by contradictory messages about people of color stemming from inconsistency between parents' verbalized beliefs and their evident behavior. As Martha explained, "The treat-everyone-alike message combined with their contradictory actions resulted in a justifiably confused little girl. Was I supposed to do what they said or what they did?"

The impact of these double messages from home went deep. Judith recounts:

> The first distinct memory I have of learning about racism was when the first Black family moved into my neighborhood next door. I was about 6 years old. My mother. She had always emphasized to me that color did not matter and that I was to treat all people as I wished to be treated by them. However, I was to discover that there was more to it than that.

I had become close friends with Marilyn, a daughter in the Black family that lived next door. Marilyn had me over to dinner and to spend the night several times, and she had dinner with my family often. Then when I asked if Marilyn spend the night, my mother said no. This was a shock. My mother seemed like a different person. I argued with her; I tried to reason and persuade. She was adamant. I felt horribly ashamed to even go over to Marilyn's house. How could I be welcome in her house when she wasn't welcome in mine? I felt so torn in two. I couldn't go against my mother; but Marilyn was my friend, and somehow I must be less of a friend to her if I couldn't reciprocate her family's generosity.

Parental acceptance of friendships with children considered "exceptions" while communicating negative attitudes toward people of color in general was another form of the double message. Paula recalled:

There were a lot of Black and Mexican American kids in the public schools I went to, but I had no contact with them. My parents had some friends of color and occasionally I got to play with their kids. I remember one Black playmate, the son of a doctor and nurse from Jamaica, and feeling that he was special because he was Black, but he wasn't like other Blacks.

Sometimes the message of one parent contradicted the message of the other. Julie wrote about her father's initiating a neighborhood petition to prevent a Chinese family from moving in, and her mother who told her "We are all God's creatures." As she got older, she was furious not only with her father's bigotry, but also with her mother's passivity, never contradicting her husband and going along with his actions. Another student described how his grandparents never let him watch TV programs with people of color as characters. His parents, although disagreeing, never openly stood up to them. When he attempted to argue with his grandparents, he received no support from his parents.

Contradictory lessons also came from church. Barbara, for example, recalls:

I went to Catholic grammar school and there participated in the yearly drive to raise money for the missions in Africa. The goal was for either a class or an individual to save $5 to send to the mission. This gave you the privilege of renaming a pagan baby with a Christian name. I'm embarrassed to tell how many babies I named.

Indirect, inadequate, or nonexistent explanations about racial issues from parents or other significant adults compounded the impact of double messages. One student recalled that when she asked her parents how come it was okay to play with Chicano kids in the streets but not invite them home, "their classic ex- cuses were 'not today,' 'I just cleaned the house,' or 'I'm tired.' I got the idea that my parents didn't like my new friends so I didn't push things."

Frank wrote that he was puzzled about why he called their Black maid by her first name when he called all other adults by their last name: "When I asked my mother why, she said it was because our maid preferred it what way. Looking back on it now, I understand the relationship of inequality that allowed me to do so. As a child, I just accepted my mother's explanation."

Often, racial issues were simply not an acceptable topic of conversation, as Ann recounted,

> Race has always been as taboo a subject in my upbringing as sex or death. Maybe even more so in many ways. It has always been an area of a lot of mystery where my direct questions were met by embarrassment, avoid- ance, or lies.

Neutralizing Conflicts. White students brought a set of beliefs that, at least on the surface, enabled them to resolve the contradictory messages and tensions of their early socialization. Several pervasive characteristics of this belief system are evident in their early comments and their writing.

1. *Not noticing.* Students had no consciousness of the realities of White privi- lege and benefits, nor of the widespread and continuing consequences of racism, expressed in objective statistics about median income, unemployment, health care, political power, and so forth. They attributed discriminatory institutional policies or practices to individual racists rather than to a systemic force, and while acknowl- edging that people of color have not yet achieved full equality, they believed that their conditions are now so much better that racism is virtually a thing of the past.

Consequently, White students also thought that all they had to do to be non- racist was to avoid making overtly bigoted comments or noticing people's skin color—in other words, to be "colorblind." One student shared a good example of this approach:

> I used to test myself when I was in high school and it was important to me that I not be prejudiced. Living in New York, I used the subway as my examination ground. Upon entering, I would check to see if I noticed that there were people of various racial backgrounds. I always failed the test and then felt very guilty about still being prejudiced.

Some colorblind students felt that to study cultural differences contributes to the problem of racism. Others espoused a self-contradictory argument: They re- jected acknowledging differences but also wanted to learn about people of color.

A colorblind stance has serious weaknesses:

- Not noticing that someone is Black, for example, denies that person a history and culture, just as only noticing that someone is Black denies individuality.
- Colorblindness obscures the reality of institutional racism by attributing the source of the problem to seeing differences rather than to a system that denies certain racial groups equitable economic and political gain.
- Colorblindness justifies withdrawal from social action by assuming that racism will cease to exist when people stop noticing racial and cultural differences.
- Colorblindness does not work. It cannot simply be imposed on the confusion, anxieties, misinformation, and misconceptions Whites have about people of color and result in constructive relationships between them.

Martha provides a telling illustration of how her confused attempts to do so backfired. Living in an all-White environment despite her "nonracist" beliefs, she describes how

> a while back, I met a very interesting Black man on an airplane. We parted with a promise to get together with our spouses. This would be a new experience for me as my social group is very homogeneous White. Eventually, we did get together and had a wonderful time. Later when talking with my husband, I realized the color difference caused me to feel distracted. I was confused, and I assumed this was due to being a racist. Otherwise, how could I explain that I had noticed the color difference. This view of myself bothered me so much that we never got together again.

A second example further exposes the racist pitfalls of colorblindness:

> After graduating from college, I was in charge of the unit in a hospital where Blacks were the ward clerks and Chicanos worked in the housekeeping department. I never questioned why Anglos filled all the positions of authority and minorities filled the lower economic roles.

2. *Ethnocentrism.* When Whites control all the institutions of a society, White "norms" become synonymous with what is natural, normal, and universal. Since students taking a colorblind stance assumed that racial and cultural background was irrelevant, they also assumed they were being nonracist if they judged everyone by the same norm even when they then found others wanting. As one preschool teacher proudly said, unwittingly exposing her racism: "I get along with

all children. I had different kinds of Blacks in my classes. I had some who didn't celebrate holidays and some wore peculiar outfits. I think they were Muslims."

Negating the reality of daily racist incidents in the lives of people of color is another pernicious element of the White students' ethnocentrism. When classmates of color related experiences with racism, White students doubted the accuracy of their perceptions. "Was it really racism?" and "Did that really happen?" were typical questions. Whites usually explain the incident based on the personality of the individual of color or the other actors in the incident, rather than on personal or institutional racism. They propose that the person of color had just "rubbed the White the wrong way," or the White involved had "had a bad day," or similar explanations. Sometimes, a White student's response negated an incident as a figment of the student of color's "too sensitive" imagination. Thus, in a variety of ways, the burden of proving and combating racism is placed on the shoulders of people of color.

Students also refused to acknowledge their Whiteness as a relevant attribute of their perspective on the world. Therefore, most considered it racist for someone to consider their Whiteness as having any impact on their perceptions of others. As one mental health worker put it, "A Chicana therapist at my agency said I couldn't understand Chicano families the way she did, but I think that is ridiculous. It's racist, too."

Ruth described how she had once met with leaders of a neighboring Black community and offered to form a Black Girl Scout troop. She felt rejected and hurt by what she considered reverse racism when they said she should work on prejudice among White Scout troops in her all-White community instead.

At the school where he taught, a Black teacher told Frank that he really did not understand the Black children he was teaching. Frank said he felt that "after all my hard work, they weren't even grateful." Indignant that they were not the ones letting race "stand in the way," these students felt absolved of making any further effort to understand the perspective of the people with whom they had interacted or to change their own behavior.

3. *Denial and ignorance about their own cultural identity.* Three-quarters of the White students knew very little about their own ethnic identity. Raised to be "melting-pot" Americans, their families had dropped the culture of their original nationality and adapted to the pattern of White Anglo-Saxon Protestant (WASP) America. These students did not see themselves as coming from a particular cultural tradition or heritage; they simply identified themselves as American and had a difficult time identifying what the elements of their culture were. Joyce, for instance, described her understanding of her family's background as:

a carbon copy of the families I lived near, went to school and attended church with. We had indeed melted into a pot of chicken, Presbyterian, pink-flesh baby doll, macaroni salad, hopscotch, Baby Jane identity. It is not necessarily saddening to have become melded culturally, but it does leave me with a somber place, a sort of unrealness about my connections to history. I also realized that while I don't know very much about my own specific French and Irish history, I do know what I learned about other cultures that taught me to dislike individuals and groups of people. With great clarity, I learned to react, classify, and reject based on any combination and permutation of skin color, hair color, sex, religious practice, eye shape, height, weight, place of origin, political practices, and social customs.

Judy put it more bluntly. The opening paragraph of her ethnic identity paper read:

"Ethnic identity?" asked my mother. "I didn't know that you had one." I felt about the same. Ethnics were people who were different from you.

However, experiencing contradictions between the emphasis on everyone being an American (and therefore being the same) and the realities of ethnic differences even among Whites also created considerable confusion for many. Ann remarked:

My family made a great point of our family being melting pot citizens of the United States. However, I had to know what to do and what not to do in Plover (Polish Catholic) and Randolph (German Protestant) in contrast to what we did at home in Brookings. I had to pretend to love potato pancakes in Plover yet never ask for them in Brookings. Remembering in which church to wear a hat, when to kneel, when to sing and not sing, making sense of the Latin, finding my place in three different liturgies and three different sets of hymn and prayer books took much work. The most difficult part of growing up in that situation was that there was no one to talk with about the differences and similarities or what I liked and disliked about the three settings. There was little opportunity for me to put together a heritage that was nurturing and real for me.

In sum, White students (with a few exceptions) shared a coherent set of assumptions about themselves and racism, regardless of their individual background and experiential history. Their childhood education left most of them either confused about people of color or believing that they were inferior to themselves. Even when parents were concerned with racial injustice, the White-centered environment in which they raised their children coupled with the double messages they communicated provided no tools for creating healthy relationships with people of color or for dealing with the difficulties that racism creates for such relationships. Moreover, they had all learned and fostered a self-image of nonracism without disturbing the benefits they received as Whites, their relationships with other Whites, or their own life-styles. They could be the "good guys" by defining the "bad guys" as Whites who were overt, intentional bigots, and by remaining unconscious of the racism inherent in their own more "humane" beliefs. They did not need to change their own behavior or take the risks involved in actively confronting racist acts to sustain their nonracist image: colorblindness was sufficient.

Yet, tensions existed under their surface assurance that relationships with people of color were okay. Frank wrote:

> I was never prejudiced because my parents weren't. . . . How surprised I was when I heard from some Chicano and Black folks that they thought I was racist. How hard it has been for me to see that. While I held all those pleasant words about Negroes and Mexican-Americans, I still couldn't speak to them or reach out. It's scary for me to admit these early memories. I don't want people to know how I think inside. It has been so easy to hide my fear of different people behind denial. It has been so easy to gloss over the stereotypes with special friends. But the fears and the stereotype are still there.

White students pay dearly in loss of self-respect when they close their eyes to incidents of racial bigotry. Ruth wrote:

> Racism is tension. I recall every awareness of racism by the corresponding feeling of embarrassment or anxiety or shame or confusion.

However, most have suppressed these memories. Frank speaks for them when he admits:

> I'm not going to think about this [racism] anymore now. I have to go to work, play, bed, eat, etc. I have important things to think about. That's how I keep it safe.

Since White society colludes with this response, most of our White students would have continued to accept and carry out racist ideology and practices in their personal and work lives without the intervention of anti-racism training.

Students of Color

Most of our students of color know from an early age that their "color" and culture make them different from being White, learning early that this difference would become problematic in their lives.

Some recall hearing these messages from their peers at school. Jon writes about his early conflict about his ethnic identity as he was growing up in Hawaii:

> My parents never introduced me to any formal Chinese cultural activity as a youngster, but my introduction to my own ethnicity was no less powerful. They had a way of interspersing ethnocentric comments into otherwise normal conversations . . . characterizing Chinese males in Hawaii as physicians, lawyers, businessmen, being affluent, and excelling in fields such as mathematics, engineering and the natural sciences. Historically, there was mention of how advanced Chinese society was in the earliest of man's recorded history.
>
> At the same time, the wealth of ethnic jokes I was hearing in elementary school amazed me. Many were directed at the Chinese in a way that pokingly negated every claim made by my parents. As a result, a dubious ambivalence characterized my feeling about my own ethnicity. There seemed to exist legitimate evidence, both historical and contemporary, that allowed me to feel pride for my ethnicity, but at the same time I felt I was the object of resentment.

Jon's awareness of contradictory messages about his ethnicity is echoed by Marissa:

> Most of the kids couldn't figure me out. "You look like a Mexican, but you sure don't talk like one. In fact, you're kind of smart," they said. This caused me considerable confusion—was there something the matter with me or, was I in fact really not Mexican?

Many students remember cogent and precise incidents of learning about racism from teachers. Ernie conveys the tremendous tension created when a respected representative of the social structure, who supposedly embodies society's principles of equity and fairness, regards a cultural characteristic of one's community as an object of ridicule:

> In 1955, I was five and my sister who was seven came home in tears one day. Why? "The teacher made fun of me. She made the class laugh at me," my sister cried. How in the world would my parents deal with a Catholic nun whom they respected, . . . because she was a Catholic nun, but whom my sister accused of teasing her because the nun thought my sister's accent was cute? They, my parents, dealt with it quietly.

Theresa relates how the attitude of her first school teacher sparked a struggle that affected her for the rest of her life:

As a child I looked forward to school believing it would be the most wonderful place. My explorations of my home and family were wearing out. I needed new horizons and new adventures where everyone would be happy, love me and give me a more interesting second home. As I entered my kindergarten class, I settled back with three or four other Mexican children who spoke only Spanish. . . . My teacher tapped me on the shoulder and said "In this classroom, you cannot speak Spanish." This was humiliating and embarrassing to me. I felt very bad; I had done something very bad.

Theresa goes on to describe the profound change in her behavior to be good in the teacher's eyes. To accomplish this, she began to deny things that she and her family believed in.

Alona, a child of Mexican immigrants, discusses the powerful conflict she felt between home and school in her childhood. Her parents were proud of their culture; her teachers denigrated it. Her parents raised her by their beliefs; her teachers criticized her behavior. Alona vividly illustrates the oppressive impact of these conflicting messages:

We belong to a strong nationalistic subculture. Neighbors and friends all spoke Spanish, because they wanted to preserve their identity. The school admonished and criticized us for speaking Spanish. Some teachers were less than tactful in their criticism. This intensified our anxiety because our parent's authority was not to be questioned and we owed allegiance to our parents. But, we did not defend ourselves when criticized because of our deference and respect for elders. We thus appeared submissive and were misinterpreted by our teachers as passive, apathetic, and without motivation. This was the beginning of a long series of adjustments for us.

Even when students couldn't recall any actual events, they still somehow learned about racism. For example, Marcia explained:

I do not remember my parents talking about color in my early years. Now it may have happened that color issues were discussed, but not in the presence of children, or if they did talk about these matters that I just did not understand what they were talking about at the time. Looking back, it occurs to me that I was never taught in school nor could I have known from experience what the word *lynch* meant, or *Jim Crow*, but later when I was to hear these words, I would know exactly what they meant.

In sum, students of color indicate that from childhood they were aware of the inconsistencies between their family's and society's messages about themselves and their people. Whether these contradictions were explicit and obvious or subtle and indirect, everyone faced them and had to deal with the discomfort that produced.

Managing Conflicting Messages. Resolving the psychological dilemma of conflicting judgments about one's value as a member of a racial and cultural group is a critical developmental task for people of color. Discrepant value messages are a lifelong experience, and the work to resolve the conflicts they create is also lifelong.

Three different but not necessarily mutually exclusive strategies for coping with this major task characterize the consciousness and behavior of our students. Although they are discussed separately, the evidence suggests that students use all three responses at various times. One adopts the dominant culture's view of one's racial group as less adequate than the majority cultural group. Another denies that society's egalitarian rhetoric contains any truth and seeks to validate the oppressive experience of people of color. The third essentially ignores the entire conflict by suppressing any thought or discussion about racist relationships.

1. *Accepting society's view.* When people of color take the dominant culture's view of themselves, they implicitly accept the negation of their humanness and are thus forced to question their own basic worth. This strategy for reducing contradictions creates new conflicts and tensions, for by buying into the belief that people of color are "bad," they are left with the problem of how to be "of color" and "good" at the same time. The preservation of self-esteem, then, becomes the source of tension. In order for individuals to be of basic worth, they must resist accepting the fact that they belong to an inferior group. Consequently, they try to become less like their own people and more like the admired group. In other words, accepting society's view pushes these individuals to locate themselves outside of the racial/ethnic group.

Luisa, a 40-year-old preschool teacher of Mexican descent, talks about this process in her own and her friends' experiences:

> We'd been trying to blend, to lose our identity, because it isn't as good as Anglo identity. We used various means to accomplish this. Rita said she dyed her hair blond. Well, I didn't have to dye my hair. Unconsciously, I simply pulled the curtains over my eyes and saw myself Angloized. When anybody spoke of Mexicans, I just simply refused to identify with that group. I was removed from all those negative things they said about Mexicans because, look, I talked the same as Whites and ate the same food . . . only it really didn't work because I was really hurting deep down inside. I had spoken Spanish before English. We ate beans and tortillas at every meal along with other Mexican dishes and, more important, my mother was born in Mexico.

James, an African American, expresses similar feelings:

> I remember always wanting to have straight hair and being jealous in a way of my sisters because our mother used to straighten theirs. But not mine. Combing it was easier, and you could make more styles, we used to think. Really it just made you more like White people—nobody ever said that but we were all thinking it.

Alana, an African American from a middle-class background, has come to a new awareness of the close connection between distancing herself from her own group and accepting victim-blaming explanations of racism. In describing her outlook before anti-racism education, she states:

> For a long time, I didn't question racism because I thought I wasn't immediately affected by it. My family didn't live in the ghetto and we were middle class and I believed that Blacks in the ghetto were responsible for their own conditions. Now I have a new kind of growing consciousness. It's not my ethnic group that needs to be fixed, it's White folks' attitudes about us that need fixing.

Adopting Whites' views of one's own group usually also includes accepting the negative characteristics and stereotypes associated with other racial/ethnic groups. Anna, for instance, writes:

> For the first three years of my life, I spoke only Spanish. Our daily fare consisted of cooked beans and other Mexican foods. Then, in order to learn English, my mother insisted that my brothers, my father, and I only speak English. She laid the next rule on us around school age: We were not Mexicans, not even Mexican-Americans. We were French, since our last name was indeed French.
>
> To my young mind it was reasonable and desirable, because my mother made Mexicans sound terrible. I began to believe that it made no difference if they were wealthy or poor, all Mexicans and Mexican Americans were dishonest, unreliable, and even deserved the contempt of Whites. Anglos were the supreme race . . . blond gods. Orientals were inhuman and took girls into slavery. Blacks were ungrateful. They should be glad they have the language of their White masters. At least they did not have to struggle to learn a language to express themselves. It has taken me a long time to recognize my prejudiced beliefs.

2. *Denying society's beliefs.* The second type of response to double messages involves denying the validity of society's rhetoric about equality. This psychological orientation resists belief in White superiority, reacts to oppression by chal-

lenging mainstream society's explanations of White domination, and attempts to recapture elements of one's group culture that domination has taken away. How do you protect your view of the beauty and strength of your people's history and tradition from the assault by ever-present oppression? Students of color may appear defensive or express anger and hostility toward Whites as they deal with the tensions of this struggle.

Kay, an African American social worker in her 30s, describes her identity by highlighting the strength and beauty of her cultural background in contrast to the horrors associated with the dominant society:

> Being Black means my heritage is African, rich in greatness. Our language is rich in meaning, our music rich in expression, our history rich in accomplishments. One cannot speak of ethnic heritage, however, without mentioning the past that White society has in our heritage. In trying to live a positive, fruitful life, we have had a plethora of horrors and crimes to struggle through and overcome. The Black heritage is the slave trade, the most despicable plight to be burdened on a race of people. My ethnic heritage is Black and White restrooms, Black and White drinking fountains, second-class schools with poor equipment and supplies, riding on the back of the bus, Jim Crow laws. It is the Ku Klux Klan burning crosses on front lawns, lynching men and boys . . . my ethnic heritage is a constant rage at the way you've been treated. It is knowing that as long as these injustices are done to any Black, they are being done to me.

Anger at the treatment of Blacks by Whites is an evident theme. Yet it is secondary to the central struggle—Kay's desire to validate her group's history—the very realities the dominant group most wants her to deny.

Awareness of the daily reality of racism and the frustration of feeling powerless to create change surfaces in Beverly's writing:

> It is very hard to say when I first realized that there was something different about being Black. I grew up in an all-Black community, and I attended majority Black schools for the most part of my formal educational experience. Although I can remember conversations of adults about White people, it was not until I was around 22 or 23 years old that I began to understand what being Black in society actually entailed. One of my more vivid memories is a trip my mother and I took to her home state, Texas.
>
> In Houston, my cousins would talk about the city and where different people lived by referring to wards. In the car, my cousins would inform me as I was going through a certain ward. What I noticed was the lower the number, the nicer the neighborhood, and that Blacks did not live in the first through the third wards. It was after this trip that I remember asking

many questions about White people, which I had never done before. Also, I have never wanted to go back to Texas because, in my mind, this situation is frustrating because it is not any better, even now, and there is not much that Black folks there can do and still stay alive.

Vivienne, a 25-year-old African American woman, describes how she consciously takes action to unshackle herself and her people by returning to her cultural essence and by teaching Black children to resist acceptance of White society's judgments of them:

In college my image of myself and my people took a change. I spent six months in East Africa. For the first time, rather than focusing on the ugliness of racism, I could spend some time thinking and learning more about the beauty of my people and the lost history. I developed a feeling of belonging which enriched me so much that I became certain that I no longer wanted to be associated with this country, but instead with Africa. The family I lived with gave me an African free name, and after that I referred to myself as an African born in America. My struggle at this point in my life is to teach Black children about their African selves.

Jon, whose childhood experiences led to ambivalent feelings about his Chinese heritage, writes how during his college years he worked to adopt a humanistic philosophy. However, by the time he reached our course in pursuance of a master's degree, Jon was critical of his earlier ways of resolving ambivalence. Now he sees the racist contradictions underlying the humanistic stance:

The myth of our common humanity is perhaps an idea we should cling to, but, at this time in my life, it is for me a myth. Make no mistake about it. Because for reasons unknown, whenever I hear the utterance "our humanity," the feeling I get is that it is a humanity based upon White ideas. So for the time being, it is a myth to which I will cling. One thing is more clear for me now. I dislike White people and I am tired of them too.

This passage illustrates Jon's anger at Whites for denying his reality—for telling him that he is something to be despised while saying to the world that the brotherhood of man is beautiful.

In summary, students of color with this perspective reject racism's false picture of their people. They hold on dearly to what they know to be true: the reality of oppression against people of color, the importance of recapturing the characteristics of their cultural history, the need to articulate the racist practices of White society. Toward Whites as perpetrators of falsity and racist practice, they express a great deal of hostility.

3. *Avoiding the conflict.* A third strategy for coping with the double messages of racism is to avoid any thought or discussion about conflicting messages regarding one's racial or ethnic group and even to act as if these conflicts do not exist. Tension underlies the resulting psychological orientation. Students exhibiting this orientation focus on themselves only as individuals, and not as members of a particular racial and ethnic group. Yet they also have to grapple with other people's responses to their group identity. They attribute discriminatory situations to individual prejudice rather than consequences of particular social relationships and socioeconomic systems.

Jean illustrates the contradictions and attempted solution of this orientation:

> During my elementary and high school days, I made many attachments to people of the White race. Part of my family tree is White, so there were no problems for me. While in junior high school, I was the only Black in all my classes for three years and the experience was a learning tool. At the same time, I always wanted a Black around so I would have someone who could identify with me. As time went on, I learned that people can identify with me no matter what ethnic background, as long as I remain myself.
>
> My ethnic identity is something about which I'm still learning. I know that my ethnic group is Black, but I don't know anything firsthand about Africans, and the White man stripped away my identity years ago. My visits to the South with my family helped me learn a great deal about my family's suffering during slavery times.

Another student, Susanna, who comes from an Asian-White family, also writes about relieving the conflicting messages by finding herself as an individual:

> My earliest recollections concerning my ethnic background are of my mother telling me stories about my grandparents on both sides. She would always mention the fact that she was a descendant of Sir Francis Light who founded an island in the Pacific. On my father's side, we hear about how our ancestor, Archduke Pita, went to England with Peter the Great.
>
> I'm not sure when I first became aware of prejudice and what form it took. I do remember the Chinese girls in my class saying I was a half-caste and I didn't even understand the term. I did not ask my mother for I believed it would embarrass her. It seemed a crime though that I was different because in the convent schools I did not quite fit in with the English girls, nor could I identify with the Asian group. But I realized that sometimes there were advantages in being mixed. Whenever a play was organized, first the English and Eurasian girls were given the major parts and the other girls had only bit parts.

By the time I reached high school, somehow it no longer mattered what race you belonged to. You were just one of the gang. When I went to England as a student, I was treated as something of a celebrity, being the only student from Asia, and everyone was interested in learning more about my country, its people, and customs. I felt comfortable being different and it was during those years that I really began to find my identity.

The inherent contradictions of the "avoiding the conflict" strategy are apparent in Susanna's description of the racial discrimination she experienced because of her identity and then deciding that being "mixed" is an advantage, in first calling herself a "celebrity" and then deciding just to be her individual self. Catherine demonstrates another form of avoidance. She stresses that no matter what obstacles are put before Blacks, family strength is the crucial variable for success:

I was born in a middle-class environment and was taught to be proud at all costs, to study hard, believe in my people, to apply myself and that I could become a leader or whatever I desired. We had a culture within a culture. We were taught social grace, music appreciation, art, ballet, and attended Black plays. We also went to the movies, but had to sit in the balcony section. I attended private schools until the fourth grade. My public school had Negro children and Negro teachers who taught us to play, love, and show respect for each other.

I also knew that Black people had an extremely hard time surviving in America. Even when we rode in segregated trains and were not permitted to eat at the same time as other passengers, we adhered to social grace and were reminded that we were as superior as the so-called mainstream race. My upbringing and heritage were so strongly taught and lived by, that the pride and determination could reach out and touch you. We felt that if you possessed those qualities and truly believed in yourself, you could achieve whatever you so desired.

Catherine does not mention Black political struggle to resist domination by Whites, nor does she show any awareness of the role class played in her family's way of life. Rather, she chooses to concentrate strictly on the issue of moral character as a means by which people can rise above the conflicts within our society. Nevertheless, institutional racism makes "progress" in life precarious—society's rewards cannot be guaranteed to your children or their children solely on the basis of individual effort. Not seeing the connection of one's own family and individual life experiences to those of one's racial group distorts historical and contemporary reality. More seriously, such an exclusive focus on the individual denies the possibility of a vision for eliminating society's racism through collective effort.

In summary, when students of color begin the semester, they bring various orientations to addressing the many contradictions racism creates in their lives and in society. None of the orientations totally resolve the contradictory messages a racist society presents. Moreover, while one particular approach may be most evident in a student's thinking, it probably represents a primary rather than a sole coping strategy. Even more important, although all three are responses to managing the contradictions within a racist society, each coping strategy creates new tensions. They all represent an acceptance of society the way it is.

CONCLUSIONS

The package of ideas, attitudes, and feelings each student brings to an anti-racism course consists of many interconnecting elements. Individuals' self-concepts and understanding of social relationships are deeply influenced by their solutions to racism, with none about to escape the internalization of misinformation about themselves, society, or each other.

Both Whites and people of color develop personal ideological responses and attempted solutions to the behavioral and moral dilemmas created by racism. The elements of these psychological and behavioral orientations are primarily influenced by the side of the oppressor-oppressed relationship into which one is born. However, because it is a complex relationship, a number of responses are possible.

The students of color displayed three distinct perspectives:

1. They accepted society's view of their group and of racism.
2. They denied society's beliefs about their group and its rhetoric about equality.
3. They avoided the conflict of contradictory messages.

Most of the Whites opted for a web of beliefs that espouse the basic equality of all humans as members of the same race and a focus on people as individuals. However, these Whites then mystified the evidence and dynamics of racism—and their part in its perpetuation—by attempting to be colorblind and, as we see in the next chapter, engaging in victim-blaming strategies. A much smaller group accepted White-supremacist rationalizations.

Although all of these perspectives enable people to function within a racist society and appear stable on the surface, they also contain internal contradictions that create unresolved tensions. Students of color are much more keenly aware of these tensions than are the Whites, though not necessarily on a conceptual level. Because they live with the realities of racism, the contradictions inherent in their solutions are constantly being exacerbated and their solutions challenged. In contrast, for the most part, the White students are not aware of the contradictions in their ideological and behavioral positions. Believing they are nonracist, they neither see nor think about racism. Thus, unless some external event shatters their equilibrium, their solutions are relatively stable.

The next chapter presents the teaching challenges and methods that move both students of color and Whites from their initial consciousness to the next phase of their journey to anti-racism. It also discusses the issues and feelings with which students grapple in the next three class sessions.

CHAPTER 4

The Second Phase:
Exposing the Contradictions

Racism is anti-human because it damages everyone's healthy development and integrity. Uncovering racism's dynamics and facing the institutional and personal contradictions it creates are vital to further growth. Therefore we must first provoke cognitive and emotional disequilibrium before we can guide students' construction of a new paradigm about society and self.

TEACHING CHALLENGES

This phase presents the most difficult and sensitive teaching challenges of the entire course. Our pedagogical stance is no longer neutral. We increasingly ask students to think critically about the beliefs and behaviors that keep them enmeshed in racist and pro-racist consciousness and behavior. We know we are asking our students to experience an intellectual and emotional crisis as they discover the truth about racism and how they have colluded with it. This is a heavy responsibility.

We take great risks as we make "on our feet" decisions about when and how to push each student further along without pushing anyone over the edge at any given moment. A delicate balance between challenging and supporting students requires careful attention to who they are. Moreover, there is no guarantee that students will respond to the discomfort of disequilibrium by moving forward; they may also hold on to or return to their initial modes of thinking and operating.

Certain group dynamics are especially challenging. Creating a learning environment for everyone means balancing the different safety needs of students who are White and those of color. In the beginning, the former want security that they will not be judged as racist no matter what they say; the latter need to know that we will not allow outrageous and hurtful comments to go by without intervention. The group can also get mired in an escalating spiral of guilt and anger, emotions that inevitably arise as students face the tragedies of racism. We must help them acknowledge these feelings, understand their sources, and then move on to using emotional energy for constructive change. Emotional confrontations in class may momentarily release feelings. Although uncomfortable, these displays of emotion in a nurturing environment are only a prelude to the far more threatening tasks of confronting oneself and creating change in the real world of work and community.

Given the complex teaching tasks of the Second Phase, the emotional risks and challenges for us as course leaders are also at their highest point. We want to stay sympathetic yet calm in the face of increased emotionalism—anger, tears, hostility to us, self-pity, guilt—so that we can guide students to the next steps in their growth. We want to provide support yet avoid rescuing a student who is struggling with hard issues and feelings. It is sometimes very difficult not to feel overwhelmed and inadequate about handling situations that arise with a student or between students. The questions "What have I unleashed?" and "Will I be able to positively facilitate it?" do come to mind. We also risk getting caught up in our own strong feelings, as students' comments and behavior arouse our unresolved issues and hurts. Facing these challenges, the greatest danger is crossing the line from teacher into using the class to work on our own emotional issues.

Vital to serving as co-teachers are such habits as paying attention to how and what we are feeling during class, how these feelings are affecting the relationship with each other, signaling to the co-teacher to handle a situation if one of us is momentarily unable to do so, and debriefing each other after class. Some days, we vow we will never teach the class again. It is also important to accept that we are not perfect and that our self-discipline will (does) occasionally weaken. We need to admit and understand any lapses, and then forgive ourselves.

ACTIVITIES

We structure course activities so that students continue to examine their experiences with racism, their own identity, and cross-racial interactions but with the introduction of a new element now: We provide a conceptual framework for reflecting on and analyzing the material, the issues, and the themes that emerge from students' stories. Particularly, we want them to explore contradictions in how they understand the nature of the relationship between themselves and the society created by racism, as well as connect internal tensions to these dynamics.

Weeks 3, 4, and 5 involve looking at the impact of racism on students' ideas and experiences, establishing definitions and analyzing forms of racism, exploring the concept of victim-blaming, and setting the parameters for action projects. Class sessions guide students to face inconsistencies in their thinking, mismatches between their beliefs and behaviors, voids in their knowledge and understanding, and an awareness of the strong feelings they may have about these contradictions.

Week 3: Uncovering Attitudes and Experiences

Two activities take place during this session: (1) a cultural questionnaire and large-group discussion, and (2) small-group discussion of "hard moments."

Two goals guide these activities: (1) to help students acknowledge the limitations of their knowledge about people of color, and (2) to help students relate their experiences with those of others in their racial/ethnic group as a prelude to connecting the collective experiences of the group to the policies and practices of society's institutions. We anticipate anxiety and discomfort, and therefore allow time and space for feelings to emerge. Yet we exercise direction and control so that confrontation does not become the center of attention and rob the environment of the degree of safety necessary for continuing disclosure of feelings.

Activity 1: Cultural Questionnaire and Discussion. At the beginning of the class, we give students the following questionnaire, which probes knowledge about nondominant cultures:

1. Within the last 3 years, approximately how many movies have you seen depicting people of color? (For students of color, use your own group or other groups.) Name three.
2. Approximately how many books have you read concerning the thought and life-styles of people of color? (Include fiction, history, political essays.) Name three that you feel had the greatest impact on you.
3. List some of the books written by people of color that you have read. Which ones would you recommend? Why?
4. List periodicals with which you are familiar that are Black/Chicano/Asian/Native American in origin and content.
5. What multicultural events have you attended?
6. Name three television shows depicting people of color and or themes about their lives.
7. Which television shows named above depict fairly accurate representatives of these groups?
8. List 10 nationally known people of color and explain their achievements.
9. List and describe the achievements of five people of color in your local community.
10. What forces do you see blocking the advancement of "ethnic/minority groups" in the United States?
11. How do you believe the learning style of African American, Chicano, Native American, and Asian children differs from that of European American children?
12. What do you believe are some things that enhance an African American, Chicano, Native American, or Asian American child's performance in the classroom? Elaborate.
13. Do you believe racism can be eliminated? Why or why not?

In a task-oriented atmosphere, students follow instructions to write responses quietly, adhere to a 20-minute time limit, and then turn in the questionnaires. Sometimes, students protest the "testing atmosphere," commenting that their memories fail them under such circumstances or that they cannot think well under such pressure. We respond by encouraging them to do their best and telling them not to worry, but we do not change the structure of the exercise.

Discussion about the questionnaire begins with this question: What were you feeling and thinking as you filled out the questionnaire? It is followed by additional oral questions:

- Why do you think you know so little about people of color? (For students of color: Why do you think so little about your own group? Why do you think so little about other groups?)
- Why are the only people of color you can name either athletes or entertainers? (If this occurs, which is often.)
- Why did you have to expand your local community to the whole state of California in order to name the achievements of five people of color?

Questions 10–13 on the questionnaire are for future reflection. We make copies of the questionnaires and return the originals to students for further discussion later in the semester.

In leading students through the cultural questionnaire, we follow these principles:

1. *Remain task-oriented.* While working on their written responses, students frequently express discomfort by giggling, whispering, asking for clarification about specific questions, raising objections, and asking for more time. We maintain the time limitations and remind students to work independently. The discomfort will be addressed in the discussion.
2. *Read body language.* We pay careful attention to students' facial expression, gestures, and body posture, and use these observations for facilitating the group discussion or to help a student express a feeling privately during break time or after class.
3. *Mediate confrontation.* During discussion, students express ignorance and embarrassment about not knowing how to answer the questions. One student may say something that upsets another student, without being aware of how aggravating the comment is. If confrontation between students starts, we take over, acknowledging but stopping the confronting party from continuing and gently probing the confrontee about the provocative comment. Students are not really ready to have their feelings and thoughts criticized, because they

are just beginning to voice them. Later in the semester the process of challenge and rebuttal is more useful.

4. *Support without rescuing.* As students admit their lack of information, embarrassment, and ignorance, there is a temptation to let them off the hook by saying, "Oh, you probably know more than you think." Instead, we acknowledge their dilemma, "Yes it is embarrassing not to be able to name Black and Brown writers," and support the notion that it is not solely their personal inadequacy at fault.

5. *Probe into deeper consciousness.* We ask: "Can you be more specific about how you feel?" "What else can you think of?" "What do you think made you feel this way?" "Do you have any other feelings?" We gently point out the contradictions in their statements. "You say you don't notice people of color in television shows but you always are aware of them in literature. How do you reconcile this?" We try to use questions that help students delve deeper, but we do not criticize.

Activity 2: Small-Group Discussion of "Hard Moments." This exercise explores students' difficult interracial encounters. White students are asked to explore their feelings about facing their personal racism, and students of color their personal encounters with racism.

We divide students into two groups for this activity—Whites in one group and students of color in another, and we explain that the purpose of the separate groups is to create an environment where free and honest sharing can occur by lessening the fear of hurting others' feelings or evoking anger or defensive denial. This strategy is similar to separating women from men to explore sexism. We ask everyone to talk only about themselves since the goal is to help everyone work through their negative feelings by uncovering and facing them, instead of allowing them to continue influencing their awareness, attitudes, and interactions at a subconscious level. We ask students not to judge others: They can ask supportive questions for clarification or further information, but judgments and prescriptions about how someone ought to have felt are not permitted. Here are helpful strategies for facilitating the "hard moments" discussions:

1. *Ensure that everyone takes a turn.* Each student should share at least one story. The most effective method is to go around the circle rather than asking for volunteers.

White students often feel threatened by their separation into a White-only discussion group. For them, the first task is to name and discuss those feelings. Typically, they first insist that separate groups are counterproductive to learning about positive interracial relations. With probing, responses also reveal fears that the students of color will criticize and make fun of them and considerable discomfort about being labeled White and therefore identified as a member of the oppressor group. As long as they are in interracial groups, White students can focus on the problems of people of color; in a White-only group, they are forced to look at what it means to be White in the context of racism. By the end of the activity, most recognize the value of the homogeneous groups.

2. *Encourage explicit personal statements.* We encourage students to discuss experiences both in and out of class that have had a strong emotional impact on them, stories they perhaps chose not to share in the racially mixed class setting.

3. *Share your own hard moments.* Since White students are often initially resistant to and uncomfortable with this activity, the White instructor opens with one of her own difficult moments interacting with a person of color and, as the discussion continues, shares others when appropriate. Doing so sets the expectations for the group, models willingness to expose oneself, and communicates the important lesson that we are all caught in the web of racism.

Students of color generally welcome the opportunity to meet together to talk about their concrete incidents of experiencing racism. We find it more useful for the instructor of color to disclose a hard moment later in the discussion. Since the homogeneous group provides a chance to express anger and frustration about racism without being interrupted by someone wanting justification or proof of the legitimacy of their perceptions, students of color inevitably also share negative feelings toward Whites. The instructor's story is often needed to keep the group from getting stuck there and to help gear their thinking toward exploring feelings about their own racial identity and to open up the topic of negative attitudes that exist between different groups of color.

4. *Probe into deeper consciousness.* Through gentle but persistent questions, we ask students to do more than just share a hard moment. We push them to look under the surface to acknowledge unpleasant emotions, uncover a fuller picture and the context of the interaction, and reveal the impact of this incident on their views about Whites and about people of color.

If students talk too much about a particular experience, we move them on politely; if they intellectualize ("hasn't there always been racism in the world?"), we bring them back to themselves ("That is not the point: what has it meant in your life?").

5. *Be nonjudgmental and supportive.* "I know this is hard, but it's important to look at uncomfortable things." We encourage students to tell their stories by listening carefully, giving no signs of disdain or disagreement about how they interpret these experiences. Listening to outrageous incidents without flinching is difficult, but self-disclosure by students is the highest priority.

6. *Introduce the concept of the social meaning of individual experiences.* After everyone has shared personal experiences, we suggest a relationship between the incidents and their feelings to the dynamics of racism and the consequences of being socialized in a racist society. We want students to understand that their behavior, feelings of fear, confusion, and anger are the result neither of their own personal inadequacies nor those of the people with whom they were interacting. Instead, they are a result of a social relationship created by institutionalized racism.

Themes to look for in the White students' discussion include fear of exposure as a racist, the differences between Whites' anxieties about people of color and the reality of their actual encounters, and fear about what other Whites will do to them if they talk out against racism. During the discussion, two dynamics should become clearer: (1) how they generalize a single difficult incident with a person of color to their global expectations for a whole group, and (2) behaviors of theirs that prevent further communication and understanding or perpetuate unequal power relationships.

For students of color, the group leader's main task is to guide them to pay attention to the strategies each has developed for coping with or confronting racist incidents. Two further themes should become clearer: (1) similarities among experiences and feelings of members of different racial and ethnic groups, resulting from their similar status as oppressed groups in this society, and (2) ways they internalize racism and participate in its perpetuation against themselves and other people of color.

Week 4: Institutional Racism

The objectives of this session are: (1) to define concepts of individual, institutional, overt, and covert racism; (2) to help students apply these concepts to their own experiences; and (3) to explore the relationship of the individual to institutional racism.

Activity 1: "The Drawbridge" Exercise. "The Drawbridge" exercise is taken from Judith H. Katz's *White Awareness: Handbook for Anti-Racism Training* (1978, pp. 70–72). It begins with an instructor reading the following story to the group:

THE DRAWBRIDGE

As he left for a visit to his outlying districts, the jealous baron warned his pretty wife: "Do not leave the castle while I am gone, or I will punish you severely when I return!"

But as the hours passed, the young baroness grew lonely, and despite her husband's warning she decided to visit her lover, who lived in the countryside nearby.

The castle was situated on an island in a wide, fast-flowing river. A drawbridge linked the island to the mainland at the narrowest point in the river.

"Surely my husband will not return before dawn," she thought, and ordered her servants to lower the drawbridge and leave it down until she returned.

After spending several pleasant hours with her lover, the baroness returned to the drawbridge, only to find it blocked by a gateman wildly waving a long, cruel knife.

"Do not attempt to cross this bridge, baroness, or I will have to kill you," he cried. "The baron ordered me to do so."

Fearing for her life, the baroness returned to her lover and asked him for help.

"Our relationship is only a romantic one," he said, "I will not help."

The baroness then sought out a boatman on the river, explained her plight to him, and asked him to take her across the river in his boat.

"I will do it, but only if you can pay my fee of five marks."

"But I have no money with me!" the baroness protested.

"That is too bad. No money, no ride," the boatman said flatly.

Her fear growing, the baroness ran crying to the home of a friend and, after explaining her desperate situation, begged for enough money to pay the boatman his fee.

"If you had not disobeyed your husband, this would not have happened," the friend said. "I will give you no money."

With dawn approaching and her last resource exhausted, the baroness returned to the bridge, in desperation attempted to cross to the castle, and was slain by the gateman. (p. 72)

After reading the story aloud, we follow the procedure described by Katz. First, we ask everyone individually to rank-order the degree of responsibility for the baroness's death of each of the characters. Small groups of five to six students then meet to try to agree about a ranking order. After approximately 30 minutes, the whole class discusses the results of the smaller group debates, the various rankings, and the different perspectives about society and social change the rankings implied.

We facilitate students in identifying contrasting views and the assumptions each view makes about the possibilities and legitimacy of action against oppressive conditions. In particular, we ask them to consider differences in the ranking of each character, when they are viewed as individuals acting apart from any societal context or as operating within the confines of imposed social relationships.

Finally, using the symbolism described by Katz (1978), we suggest to the class that the characters in the story can be equated with social forces in contemporary society: The baron becomes the symbol for White society; the baroness, for people of color; the gateman, the police force and military; the boatman, White institutions; the friend, liberals; and the lover, enticements such as the Declaration of Independence, the U.S. Constitution, and other American ideals of freedom (p. 70). We then ask students to reconsider ranking the characters in light of the new symbolization and in light of present-day conditions. This part of the discussion deepens consideration of the responsibility for maintaining or changing oppressive conditions, and the power or powerlessness of the victim in self-determination and in effecting social change.

As students argue for their particular view, they become clearer about their own perception of the relationship between the individual and society. For most, this activity is fun and nonthreatening because it centers on a fictitious historical situation. Nevertheless, when contemporary social relationships are discussed during the last part of the activity, some students do experience discomfort. They are faced with the recognition that, from the perspective of the victim, current societal rules and relationships cannot be accepted if change is to occur for them.

Activity 2: Definitions and Forms of Racism. We begin with a lecture based on the following institutional racism outline, which is displayed on a large easel or chalkboard:

    I. Definitions
       A. Prejudice: belief in stereotypes
       B. Bigotry: belief in White supremacy
       C. Racism: attitude or action whose outcome oppresses people of color and benefits White people, regardless of stated intent
       D. White privilege: the consequences of historical institutionalized racism; the benefits that Whites receive (economic, social, cultural, political)
    II. Forms of racism paradigm
       A. Individual: one person
       B. Institutional: organized groups of people
       C. Overt: intentional and conscious, where behavior and beliefs are congruent
       D. Covert: unintentional or unconscious, where behavior and beliefs are incongruent

After responding to student questions about the points in the lecture, we ask students to meet in small groups to identify and generate examples for each form of racism (see Figure 4.1) and to share their reactions to the conceptual framework. Then the class reconvenes, and each group shares briefly its examples and reactions to the conceptual framework, while the instructor writes them into the outline of the forms of racism paradigm.

The objective criteria postulated by the four-way categorization of the forms of racism challenges students to consider the scope, depth, and pervasiveness of racism. On the one hand, this leads them to identify how they have acted in racist or pro-racist ways even when unaware of doing so. On the other hand, they gain insights about how their own attitudes and behavior are consequences of social forces beyond their own personalities and personal backgrounds.

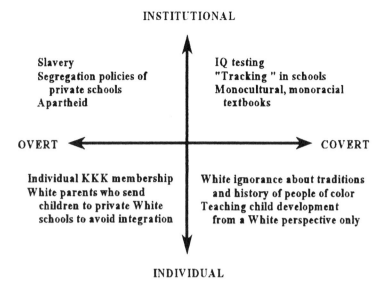

INSTITUTIONAL

Slavery
Segregation policies of
    private schools
Apartheid

IQ testing
"Tracking " in schools
Monocultural, monoracial
    textbooks

OVERT ⟵——————————⟶ COVERT

Individual KKK membership
White parents who send
    children to private White
    schools to avoid integration

White ignorance about traditions
    and history of people of color
Teaching child development
    from a White perspective only

INDIVIDUAL

FIGURE 4.1. Examples of Forms of Racism

Introducing the concept of institutional racism at this time is critical. If it is presented earlier in the semester, students could use the information inappropriately as a tool to avoid probing personal attitudes and feelings. After they confront their personal feelings and experiences, however, the concept of institutional racism helps expand their awareness that it is more than an individual issue. The analysis leaves White students without a way to think of themselves as nonracist and, for students of color, either shatters attempts to deny racism or reinforces their sense that racism is indeed systemic.

Facilitating class activities at this point in the course must follow two guidelines:

1. *Stress the conceptual.* Don't let students get stuck on personalizing specific examples of racism. Stress the four core concepts underlying specific examples—individual and institutional and overt and covert racism. For instance, the example of a White family moving out of a neighborhood that is becoming racially mixed may prompt the following reaction: "Well I did that and I don't think that I'm racist. My kids needed a better school." A suitable reply is, "I don't question your motives, but when we look at the consequences of the move, we see 'White flight.'" Alternatively, a teacher who uses IQ testing may say, "I didn't choose to. It's part of my job." In reply, we point out, "Regardless of your reason, the consequences for children of color are the same."

2. *Probe for comments.* When no one comments on the framework (delineated in Figure 4.1), it is usually a sign of resistance. So we ask directly, "Is anyone having trouble with this?" It is important to uncover students' confusion and disagreement with our analysis. The concept of institutional racism may challenge the dominant notion of racism as individual bigotry and prejudices and not institutional structures. The concept of covert or "unintentional" racism usually reveals the most emotional difficulty. It may be necessary to help students recognize their discomfort and recognize that wishing not be racist is insufficient grounds for changing the definition.

Week 5: Action Projects and Victim-Blaming

The two activities for this session turn students' attention to strategies for addressing and eliminating racist practices in their work as educators, counselors, nurses, and other human service professionals.

Activity 1: Action Project. By the fifth week, students are ready to design an action project. This project requires students to take a public anti-racist stand in their workplace or community, thus engaging the behavioral dimension of learning to be anti-racist.

Students will not eliminate racism in America through their projects, but they will take steps toward active anti-racism. Unsuccessful projects, therefore, are not those that fail to achieve their desired outcome (for one can learn as much from such failure as from success); rather they are those that students failed to undertake. Not doing an action project means an incomplete for the class.

A wide range of projects is permissible, and concrete examples are provided. We encourage Whites to work with other Whites where possible to counter the tendency to want to work with people of color rather then confront issues of racism in their own community. We also encourage a wide range of styles of work, wanting students to choose an issue and a strategy that are both personally meaningful and useful in their particular setting. However, we do insist that they work with adults, rather than focusing their efforts solely on children or youth. On rare occasions, when we judge a student to be very unready to deal publicly with the issue of racism, we permit research as a project. Students are given written guidance to help them choose an action project (see Figure 4.2).

At the beginning of this session, we quickly go around the room asking students to describe briefly the action projects they have been thinking about doing. Then we divide the class into groups of 8–10 people based on common areas of interest. For example, those wishing to develop classroom-based projects would meet together, while those working with adult or community organizations would form another group. Called "support groups," these meet together periodically until the semester ends. The responsibility of the support group is to help members refine and implement their action projects, provide opportunities to share

FIGURE 4.2. Action or Advocacy Project: A Reproducible Handout for Students

An action project is defined as work that involves anti-racist/multicultural advocacy and organizing for change. It can take many different forms and, of necessity, will focus on only a small part of one of the numerous possible areas that need change. Action projects can be:

Advocacy and Organizing at Work. This involves action that will either change present practices or implement a new program that will move your place of work closer to a pluralistic approach to working with children and families. If you choose to work in a setting serving children, you must also include adults (i.e.. the children's parents or fellow teachers).

Community Organizing. You can either participate in advocating/organizing or conduct a "shadow study" of an advocacy/action group whose work includes anti-racism/multicultural issues. There are many community organizations working on a wide assortment of issues relevant to the issues raised by this course. As you identify the area in which you are interested, your instructors can help you choose a group with which you would like to work or learn.

Action Research. Research an issue that affects children and use the data you gather for some specific action. Here are suggestions:

- Search the children's library of your school or community for books that authentically portray children of color *and* for books that convey stereo-typical and racist messages. Then use this information to work with the librarian, parents and neighbors, so that improvements can be made in the quality of books available to children.

- Develop a curriculum unit for children about people who have struggled against racism, including Whites and people of color.

- Research child development and psychology textbooks for inclusion of multicultural material and information about how children develop racial identity and awareness.

Good Ideas for Selecting Student Action Projects. Some things to consider in choosing your project:

- What is bothering you a lot?
- With whom do you want to work?
- What is your preferred work style?
- What seems "doable?"

The hardest aspect of being a change agent is to choose one specific issue from the many things you feel need to change, and then to focus on specific enough goals so that a plan of action can be developed and implemented.

After You Have Completed Your Project ...

Write to publishers and professional organizations to publicize your results. Also, encourage others in your profession to launch their own action projects.

and overcome fears, and gain feedback and suggestions from classmates about their work. Moreover, describing one's social-change efforts to a group of peers represents a public commitment to take action.

The instructors provide written questions to guide peer group discussions, and then they circulate, dropping in and out of support group interactions, answering questions, making suggestions, and providing direction. The written questions for action projects are as follows:

1. Who/what are you specifically trying to change? Change to what?
2. What forms of racism will you be dealing with?
3. What is the organizational nature of the group or institution you want to change: peers, clients, people who are organizationally below or above you?
4. What specific strategies will you use? What resources and tools will you need?
5. What or who will be obstacles to your success? What or who will be supportive?
6. How will you know when you have achieved your goals?

While peer support is useful in getting people started, most students also require help from instructors, particularly in defining a project that is specific and manageable enough to be completed during the semester. Frequent individual conferences are scheduled to help students develop a plan of action.

Students' problems about what might constitute a viable action project generally fall into one of four categories:

1. *They have no idea where to start.* "I can't think of anything." We start by asking questions to uncover some ideas, What interests you? What are you concerned about? Where do you work and live? What are some of the burning problems for you in these settings? If nothing can be uncovered with such questions, we identify some examples of action possibilities: "Well, given your life, here are some concrete things I think you can do. . . . Do any of these ideas interest you?" We also give students time to consider further options, saying "Take a week to think about it."
2. *They have a general idea about what to do but are foggy about the details and the specific strategies.* "I want to do something about the schools." We ask them about their goals, What do you want to change? Using the guide sheet of questions, we focus them on narrowing their ideas to something concrete and doable.
3. *They pick a project that is unacceptable.* It either (1) is not related to racism (e.g., "I want to make the city government install access ramps for wheelchairs at city hall"), (2) is "missionary" in intent (e.g., "I think I want to teach low-

income Black parents skills in parenting"), or (3) solely addresses an individual attitude (e.g., "I want to change my father's bigoted attitudes"). We remind students that the project must deal with racism as a primary focus, although other "isms" might be attacked in the process. We also stress that Whites must work with Whites who have the power to perpetuate the social conditions, and not only with the targets of those conditions. And although only one person may change as a result of their efforts, more than one person must be the target of change.

Activity 2: Lecture on Blaming the Victim. The second half of this class is devoted to a critique of "victim-blaming ideology" (Ryan, 1976), a way of thinking that permeates social science theory and research and whose logic forms the basis for many human service programs (see Chapter 1). A lecture and discussion build on the reading assignment of Ryan's book and provide new information so students can relate victim-blaming to their own ideas and work experiences.

After the instructors lay out the steps of Ryan's (1976) hypothesis, the discussion examines what these mean in the thinking and action of the class participants. The class addresses such discussion questions as:

- How did reading Ryan's book make you feel?
- In your own words, what do you understand Ryan to say?
- Does the victim-blaming process occur in any of the settings where you work or live?

We then ask students to form small groups and create a victim-blaming solution and a non–victim-blaming solution to a scenario such as the following:

> You know a mother of a baby with a disability who has been offered occupational therapy through a local government-sponsored program. The mother expressed an interest in getting help for her baby but has not gone to the first two appointments. How would a victim-blamer respond to this situation? What would be a non–victim-blaming response?

In this small-group activity, victim-blamers argue that the mother does not really care and would plan a way to "motivate" her to take care of her children. Non–victim-blamers look for constraints in the mother's social/political context that prevent easy access to proper care for her family and thus plan a way to rearrange the service delivery system.

The victim-blaming discussions generate considerable tension. We find that students who want to discount each example of victim-blaming will irritate other students who find the analysis illuminating. Unless the underlying issues are articulated and examined, group interaction can become counterproductive. We find that these approaches to guiding the group discussion are helpful:

1. *Zero in on defensiveness*. Typically those students who are defensive are not conscious that they are indirectly invalidating and trivializing the situations in which "victims" find themselves. They claim they are simply asking questions for clarification. (And of course, some questions really are just that—but others are more loaded.) Thus, when students of color express anger and level accusations of racism, White students can become even more defensive, decreasing productive communication. When this happens, we take time out from the "intellectual" discussion of victim-blaming to acknowledge the affective responses so that they do not interfere with students' ability to listen and to evaluate new ideas. Students meet in groups of two, where each person has a designated amount of time (e.g., 5 minutes) to talk about feelings while the other person listens without interruption or judgment. If needed, a further extension of this activity is to ask a few students to share what they learned, and then return to the discussion topic.

2. *Facilitate confrontation*. Now, helping students work through confrontations is very useful. We want students to put their ideas out in the open, learn to verbally struggle with others, and avoid withdrawal. But because it is almost "instinctive" for many instructors to want to avoid confrontation, perhaps out of fear that things will get out of hand, the tendency is to rescue the class with comments that smooth things over: "Are you really both saying the same things, just using different words?"

   Instead, when a confrontation occurs, we make sure each person in the interaction gets turns to have a full say before others are allowed into the discussion. We let discussion go on as long as it is useful both in terms of the individuals involved and the rest of the class. Strong confrontations have a powerful impact on the class as a whole, so after conclusion of a confrontation, we have students meet in dyads to discuss their feelings.

   Once the class is reconvened, we engage students in a discussion with such questions as: What issues were involved in the different perspectives? What did you learn? What was gained? Do you have clarity about the two perspectives and, moreover, about the origin of the two perspectives? Discussion does not necessarily mean gaining closure on the issue, but it does help students see the value in having this kind of experience.

Most students, at least in the beginning, want conversations about racism to be polite and reasonable, according to their definition of these terms. Notwithstanding, racism is neither reasonable nor polite. Students must be prepared to cope with their own feelings and with the feelings they will encounter when they go out into the world and confront racism in others. Passion is at the crux of the issue and is an integral and appropriate element in becoming anti-racist.

STUDENT RESPONSES

In this phase of the course, students examine their assumptions and experiences in the context of the conceptual framework, the readings, and class discussions. They sharpen their awareness of racism's contradictions in American life generally and in their own lives specifically. This process plunges them into the painful process of examining their situation and facing their own unresolved issues:

> At the beginning of the semester, although I couldn't say it or admit it then, I started to "feel" the lie that I had lived so long. I was terribly afraid that I was going to be exposed to something I didn't want to hear. But I knew it was time to face it even though I wasn't ready.

Many journals begin reflecting an anticipation that something powerful and necessary is imminent. Soon, the breadth of feelings being aroused also appears.

Students of Color

Key struggles for students of color focus on issues that the course raises during the first 2 weeks of this phase: reexamination of their group identity, their relationship to Whites and society's explanations of racism, their relationships with other groups of color, and their role in social change.

Reexamining Extended Group Identity. While all students of color deal with this issue, the struggle is most profound for students who have accepted society's view of their group or who have denied a group identity altogether, as they face what they have done to themselves. The emotions released in this process are extraordinary. Students write about this experience at length in their journals or want to engage others in repeated conversations. Lia describes the impact of opening herself to reexamining her group identity:

> When a Chicana introduced herself, I first felt the shock, then fear, then anger. I have had many of the experiences she related but never dared to tell anyone. My self-esteem is beginning to shatter. I've denied some things about myself and my people.

John goes into more detail:

> Even since the first night of class, I have been undergoing a deep, painful self-examination of who I really am and why I had chosen to be an all-White personality all of my life. A self-identity process has begun. I am not an Anglo—I am a Mexican! The difficult and interesting part is that I am unable to separate my ethnic race from my self-esteem. It goes

together; it is who I am; it is my EGO. I had not accepted who I really am. Anger set in when I think how futile my reaching out to Whites has been. In fact I'm often received as a threat. I, therefore, feel alienated—not really belonging to anyone. I am grieved, sad, and shocked to say that I have been anti-Mexican.

Students become extremely vulnerable. Some describe a general state of "nerves":

For the entire last week I found myself seeing things differently and more critically, and many questions formed in my mind. At first I was a little puzzled and annoyed at myself. But then I began to accept reality. I became emotional—upset at little things, seeing racism everywhere and becoming furious. I was even impatient with my family. My nerves just seem to be a wreck.

Others find their physical well-being affected: "Ever since my new race aware-ness I have been getting sick—first diarrhea, then a severe sinus condition, and yesterday laryngitis. It looks to me all psychological." Some wonder how the dominant society will now respond to them: "As long as I stayed Anglo, I knew how to interact socially and whom to interact with. As a Chicana, I'm no sure. . . . Will they accept me?"

Students also become extremely sensitive to how they are perceived or how they might be perceived by members of their own ethnic group. Maria strongly captures the tension that occurs, based on an incident she had experienced in class:

Tonight I was devastated. One of the members of our homogeneous group talked about me, saying "she doesn't know where she's at—she better get her shit together and decide whether she's Mexican or not!" How could one of ours have anything but close bonds toward me and everyone in the group? We are together in this—we need each other for support. I felt a part of the group and I felt their feelings. I thought they felt mine. But no! Homogeneous, Hell!!! Maybe I didn't make all my feelings clear and maybe I'm not sure that this class is the forum I personally care to use to make a declaration to the world.

Barbara also writes of her sensitivity about her group's views of her:

Last night I had a dream about the class. Toward the end of the evening I asked my homogeneous group for a distinction between historians and history writers. For some reason my question was answered by someone saying that I needed to look in Black history books and study Black leaders. My question was misunderstood. I wonder if the people in my ethnic group think that I am devoid of knowledge of my Black past?

Some students resist or mask the anxieties of reexamining their extended identities by disassociating themselves. Thus, Rhonda writes as if she has no shared identity with the group of Blacks who have tried to get away from their Blackness:

> Have I got a job on my hands! This class is a real challenge. I want to do something related to Black people. Because I am Black. However, I want it directed toward the so-called American Negroes—those who are consciously dead to their true identity. Those Negroes who are racist toward Blacks.

New insights also begin to appear. Pondering where to put the blame for the oppression she experienced as a child, Alana explains:

> As the years pass, I've understood how my mother is a victim of this society even more than I. So I've stopped blaming her for not letting us speak Spanish once we became of school age, and for working hard to learn how to cook "Americano." She felt the urgency of Angloizing us as quickly as possible. She could have been deported. She came over the border on a 6-month visa and that was 55 years ago! My God, how tough that must have been on her!

Reexamining Relationships with Whites and Racist Institutions. Another central struggle for students of color is the issue of relating to Whites. The description of institutional racism validates what they know—that racism still exists (even if they have been suppressing this knowledge). They were not being paranoid all the times they felt rejected or ignored, and they are not entirely responsible for this situation. To reaffirm these realities, however, is bittersweet. Moreover, the reluctance of White classmates to admit to themselves their role in perpetuating racism and their inability or unwillingness to understand the consequences of racism for people of color spark anger. Perhaps rage is a better word. Jon captures the essence of this reaction: "These White people in this class are really having a hard time with the issues. When are they going to admit they're racists?"

Their anger is not so much about the condition of the oppressed as it is about the absence of understanding by Whites of that condition. For example, Kay writes:

> I was infuriated by the lack of concern of some people. It was really upsetting that after the racism of [the folk tale] *Black Sambo*, White folks still think that the story is "neat." Remember, you're not Black! Nothing can be at the same time, both racist and "neat"!

Students of color were also angered by those White students who said they were being victimized whenever their racist behavior or attitudes were challenged. Barbara muses:

I wonder why should we as people of color try to tell White folk anything since they seem to turn deaf ears? When I pointed out to one student how I felt about her racist comments, I was accused of attacking her. People acted like I had committed a crime. Although another White student was very supportive of me and pointed out that because of the class's reaction to my comment I had been overlooked and my feelings shown no concern, the Whites basically clamored in protection of the White student. Rights were the issue and the protection thereof. When are OUR RIGHTS GOING TO BE RECOGNIZED?

While the depth of their anger appears in students' writing, it is rarely seen in actual class interactions. At this point in the semester, we see relatively polite confrontations. This reflects a mediating concern for students of color—fear of becoming too angry. This is especially true for the students who believe that they or their families "made it" by themselves and who have heretofore accepted society's conception of their racial/ethnic group. Rhonda illustrates this struggle to control feelings, even in the private moment of reading about the conditions of Black people:

I found this book hard for me to read because many personal feelings came up, and I didn't want to read anymore. At this point, I'm wondering how much of me is invested in the Black revolution? There's too much violence and anger, and I already have enough anger in me without subjecting myself to more.

Others are afraid to let their anger erupt because they fear their behavior will resemble militant anti-White Blacks: "I'm holding the anger back. I want to say more but what if I do; then what? I don't want people to be afraid of me or discount me or worse."

As they consciously face the pervasiveness and subtleties of racism in their lives, students of color become more sensitive to situations where they feel their perspective is being denied. Johanna writes:

This past Monday I asserted myself and said that I had been feeling some racist behavior on the part of the White, blue-eyed janitor. The director interrupted me and wouldn't allow me to finish, saying, "Well maybe you did something to provoke it." Prior to this she had reminded us that we were here to support one another and nurture each other. I responded to her reply by saying, "When I point this out about the janitor, it doesn't mean that I want to do him in but that I expect to be heard and understood with staff support." Her reply: "I'll buy that." Not a very good answer, and it certainly didn't make me feel any better.

The class becomes an arena for blowing off steam and for being believed:

> I use the classes a great deal to check out my own sanity and to get emotional support from other Blacks for dealing with my own frustration, anger, and hurt. The classes give me a "safe" place to ventilate these powerful feelings. They also validate them, which helps me maintain a sense of self-confidence in my own knowledge and understanding which is continuously questioned in my relationships outside this class.

Reexamining Relationships with Other Groups of Color. As students re-examine how they have dealt with their extended group identity, some want to draw sharp lines around what they consider exclusive to their group. It is as if the elimination of outsiders protects the newly developing ability to express one's own way of seeing life experiences. Competition among students of color for "center stage" in the discussion about racism also emerges. So too do examples of mis-understanding and biases toward other groups of color. One African American student's journal reflects what many others stated:

> One thing I've noticed this semester is that we've dealt very little with subject matter on Blacks. The most oppressed, repressed people of people has not truly been touched upon. We've seen films on the Latino migrant workers, had class discussions on the Latino vs. the American culture, and viewed a film on the El Salvadoran problem. The Blacks are in America. If we want to discuss racism, we have that here . . . with Blacks. And the racism toward other races? Well, they probably chose to come here to America for whatever reason they had. Blacks were dragged, beaten, pushed, pulled, lied to, and tricked to get them on that slave ship. They didn't hop on deciding to go to the land of the free and home of the brave with hope for a better tomorrow.

Latino students express a similar sentiment in relation to their group:

> There's injustice in this class in the fact that the topic of Brown people has been excluded. I don't know. Maybe I'm discontented because I just heard a Chavez speech. It was mind-boggling. And then, too, having a Black teacher; she could feel more compelled to concentrate in that area. After all, we live in California and we should touch on racism here. Yes, there is racism in other countries, and yes, other minorities are abused in America. But racism in other countries is over there and we're here! California was stolen from Mexico!

These reactions are explored in the people of color "homogeneous group." Guided discussions help them admit to their ambivalence about each other, their lack of information, and the stereotypes they have learned about each other. Exploration of these beliefs offers them a larger picture of institutional racism and reduces the tension among the groups of color. An Asian American student writes:

> Our discussion about "cholos" was fascinating. I realized how biased my view of Mexicans was, partly from my lack of firsthand experiences with them, but also from the little interaction I have had. I know that nobody ever told me bad things about them, nobody in my family, but my impressions are the same as most Whites, I guess, because of the cars I see with Mexican youth in them, and so forth. What blew my mind is how unconscious I was about these attitudes and now I feel guilty for being sucked into the whole racist scheme.

Another student puts it succinctly:

> I was wondering if I would have any revelations in this class because so far it has just confirmed what I already know about racism. But wow, what I didn't know about my own prejudices.

Homogeneous group discussion also enables students of color to explore both their common experiences and the differences in how racism affects their groups, while avoiding ranking one as more oppressed than another. Gradually, a new sense of their common interests begins to emerge:

> The discussions of racist incidents brings forth much pain when we come to the subject of our children and education. I've experienced many negative attitudes and behaviors concerning my daughter and her abilities, and discussing this treatment we've received from the schools makes me angry and upset. It's interesting to hear that so many of the minority parents in this class have experienced the same frustrations within the school system.

Reexamining Their Role in Social Change. The toughest challenge for students of color is seeing the connection between the larger issues of a racist society and their own individual behavior. Expressing their anger toward Whites in their journals and informal interchanges with each other provides only transitory satisfaction. They may "feel better," but being "pissed at White folk" does not resolve the basic conflict or ease their central struggle: How do they change the arrangement of a society that acts to negate their development? Evidence of an examination of their own activity in the struggle for change begins to appear. For instance, Karen writes: "Reading these books makes me so mad. When are we going to stop letting ourselves be victimized?"

Others question their own inactivity. Rachel reflects the introspection this process stimulates:

I am suspicious of conformity, yet I know I need, for my own involvement and continuing growth and humanness, to identify with some relatively like-minded group or individuals. So I guess I'd say not seeing and acknowledging the possibility of choices is a slave mentality. I feel guilty at times for not being more verbal or more active, and I sometimes think that guilt serves two purposes. It is a signal that something I've done isn't consistent with how I feel I ought to be. But the other is a kind of deadening junction that keeps me from taking action. Not taking action means I'm afraid of the consequences; so I try and figure out what the consequences of action might be. Of course, I usually can't guess at what the consequences might be, and then I just either have to drive in or hold back. The bottom line though seems to be fear of rejection if I act.

A week later, further insights appear:

I don't think I fear rejection as much as I think I fear the consequences of my actions. A short time before Dr. King was shot, he said that when people conquered the fear of death nothing could hold them from their convictions. He stated that he no longer was afraid of dying, therefore he went on to fight for what he felt was right. When I can look death in the face as he did, I feel I will be able to carry on with my fight.

Some students struggle with seeing their efforts as inconsequential:

Being reminded of the "status of Black people in the 1980s" just wipes me out emotionally. I can hardly bear to think about all the work of the 1960s that we did; all the marching, all the sitting in, all the dying. . . . Look what it got us.

However, many also ask themselves, as does Kim, "How can I do more, even one small person?" In sum, students of color begin to examine the consequences of their own internalized oppression and to uncover the how and why of their reactions to others and to themselves. In the next chapter, we will return to a discussion of how students of color manage their feelings and transform their reactions by taking a pro-active role.

White Students

Finding out how racism really works is shocking and provokes and intensifies both the introspection and the conflict of White students. Judy's pithy comment, "It is like ripping away a veil that has been in front of my eyes all my life," typifies the feeling of many of her classmates.

Facing Institutional Racism and White Privilege. The concept of systemic racism is new for most White students, and a powerful discovery. Some try to put off the discomfort. During the fourth week of the course, for example, one student admits:

> Yesterday when I finally got myself involved in the reading and writing, I realized what the difficulty had been for me. The subject is really painful and one I haven't given a lot of previous in-depth thought to. One of the really uncomfortable things for me is that all this is pointing up how much worse the racial situation is that I ever thought it was.

Others, like Ann, describe a progression of increasingly strong responses:

> When I attended the first class, I couldn't believe the honest self-disclosure of everyone. I was overwhelmed by hearing people talk about their backgrounds and experiences. I deal with emotions every day, but I find it hard to put into book words what I was feeling as we went from one individual to the other. From a Black who was struggling with her identity to a White from an upper middle class Southern background; from an atheist to a Jewish rabbi; from a person proud of a lost background and history to a Mexican who couldn't understand prejudice in the United States. By the second class I felt out of place. What I thought was "the brown-skins don't like us Whites," taking it very personally. By the next week [third], when the class divided into two groups, Whites and people of color, I felt guilty for being White and part of the oppressor group that wants all the power with no room for anyone who was different. Then when we shared with the whole class, I was ashamed that I was part of the group who has institutionalized racism and hatred toward minorities.

Others also write about their feelings of shame and guilt:

> Tonight's lecture about personal and institutional racism was an eye-opener. I was surprised to see White racism in White privilege. I really and honestly never thought that because I am White I enjoyed benefits that a non-White person might not. It's sort of stepping into another's shoes and feeling like a rat. I am ashamed of my race for the destruction of culture, property, and pride of other races.

However, some, like Linda, express anger against the co-teachers for "shattering their illusions":

I was so angry last week [third class] at Carol and Louise. Was it because the truth hurt so I wanted to reject it? I suppose I enjoy looking upon my childhood and family life as a fairy tale and that all those close to me were perfect. This class is shattering my illusions and it's hard to accept.

Once people accept the reality of institutional racism, they struggle with their part in perpetuating it, as Frances movingly describes:

One of the things I found most difficult was accepting responsibility of my own racism. I've been feeling guilty, angry, and frustrated. I feel guilty because I had thoughts that were racist, laughed at jokes that were racist, and taught racism to children every year without an understanding of what I was doing.

I feel angry because no one guided me away from racism. Surely my parents should have known better. I feel angry because the very educational system I work for never taught me the truth about people of other cultures, and the university system never trained me to teach students of different cultural backgrounds.

I am angry that I was programmed to fear and despise others because their skin is dark, and angry that it is expected of me as a White woman to confine myself to White relationships and that life is arranged for me in a way that doing anything different requires a determined, sustained effort.

Exposing the underlying racism of practicing victim-blaming also has a shattering effect. Believing that they were helping people hurt by racism, they now discover that, instead, they were often colluding in their oppression. Martha describes her confusion and defensiveness after reading the required book *Blaming the Victim* (Ryan, 1976):

This is putting holes in all my beliefs. We just keep going on trying to help and often that help is just continuing things just the way they are. I'm feeling sort of lost and like I can't do anything. How do I know if what I'm doing is based on a victim-blaming approach? Boy am I confused.

Don faces the influence the victim-blaming mentality has had on him:

I can't believe I so completely fell into this [way of thinking]. When Ryan talks about victim-blamers, I realize that's exactly what I have been taught. When he talks about the worthy and the unworthy poor, the unworthy being unwed moms, etc., my gut-level reaction is "yes, that's right," even though my head tells me I shouldn't be feeling that way. It sure has produced guilt.

Amanda critically applies her new perspective to her work:

> Last week I realized that I had spent a lot of time in programs that did victim-blaming. I'd always liked to think of myself as being different and realize that I wasn't. How can I change things in a bigger way? All of a sudden now I'm feeling racism is at the root of everything—of all the evils. I'm feeling like a babe in the woods learning how to work really effectively.

Facing New Interpersonal Dynamics with People of Color. Uncovering their misinformation, confusion, and prejudice in front of classmates of color and hearing the latter's pain and anger about racism can be initially very threatening. This behavior reversed normative expectations of behavior—where the oppressed keep quiet about their problems and the oppressors do not expose their weaknesses. Martha muses about this dynamic and gains new insight about herself:

> The other night, M. [a Chicana student] said to me, "I just don't understand why you're taking this class. You say your life up there is very comfortable." This bothered me a lot because it's a question I've been asking myself. I guess I really did feel attacked by her, because I got defensive. I feel guilty at times because I've never been oppressed or denied anything because of my race (maybe as a woman). I didn't like giving her an explanation at all, but felt that perhaps she was just interested and not being accusatory. Now I'm worried about how I must come across in class.

Most White students arrive wanting conversations about racism to be polite and reasonable, according to their definitions of those terms. They have great difficulty hearing the anger about racism expressed by students of color, feeling personally attacked. They try to delegitimize this anger and even blame anger about racism for interfering with interracial harmony, rather than their own behavior or the system of racism itself. For example, after the third week, Samantha complained that

> some people of color in the class seem distant, angry, and even at times superior to the Whites. The hostility seems to be a barrier to our class and to problem-solving in the world. What irks me is that some people carry a chip on their shoulders. We all have experienced pain and humiliation, but it feels like when some Black people are with White people, they are keeping the old wounds open. Of course there are White people who work at keeping the color line drawn, but some people, both Black and White, should be able to get past that.

Why do Whites feel so threatened? Many write during these weeks about wanting to be sure that people of color will not criticize or accuse them of racist attitudes as a precondition to their speaking in class. In other words, they expect the people of color to tolerate the pain caused by racist statements but do not want to experience any discomfort themselves. Underlying this attitude is a *Catch 22* situation: "Don't undermine my self-image as a nonracist; if you do, then I won't work on becoming anti-racist."

Judy describes her anxiety when the class meets in homogeneous groups:

> My dark-skinned classmates are together to share their experiences with racism and how they survive in a culture dominated by people who look like me. I feel left out, excluded from the oppressed minority. Is it my fault I haven't been oppressed for my skin color? When we started talking as a White group, I realized other people were as worried about what the other group was saying about us. When we heard laughter, we were sure it was at our expense.

Later, Judy communicated her worry to classmates of color, and found out that they had neither talked nor laughed about the Whites. Her response further illustrates her need for reassurance: "Are you sure there is no hostility coming from your side helping me to feel paranoid? How can I look at my racism, my conditioning, my background? How can I open up if I don't feel you listen and not blame?"

White students' demands that they be neither criticized nor rejected triggers resentment, frustration, and anger in students of color. As one Black student explained: "Whites expect us to be vulnerable and to be open about our lives and feelings, but they don't want to be vulnerable themselves. They just want to intellectualize about racism." "The Whites' defensiveness is a big burden," writes a Chicano student:

> It takes me a couple of days to unwind from this class. Why must we always be the ones who have to be sensitive and considerate? Being angry at racism and at Whites for their racism is not anti-White in general, even though it may be perceived that way. Sometimes I feel that they are never going to change.

Gradually, students gain insights about their contradictory desire for growth without risk—a crucial step towards anti-racism. For example, Samantha admits to herself:

> I've been more or less scared of people of color all my life, and I still am. I don't want to be, and I'm here to try and figure out how to change. But I

realize that I want to do it real easily. I want to be able to say now I'm anti-racist and to be immediately accepted—but I am also recognizing that it can't happen like that. Will I ever find my way through this mire?

Janine articulates the complexities of the journey:

I have never in my life before experienced the intensity of anger like June's. I did not assume that her anger was directed at me personally; even so, it seemed devastating. I understand that June and all Blacks have been deeply hurt. I have more trouble understanding her lashing out at a roomful of people who are choosing not to be racist and genuinely trying to learn and help in the cause of justice. The other side of this, I recognize, is that Whites say things that reveal racist attitudes. I wish that the motiva-tion of choosing to grow in this area could diffuse the anger. Maybe all of these feelings come under the category of self-pity, which I want to leave behind. I continue to be frustrated, though. When I now see the problem, I feel very limited by my own White middle-class thinking to see any solution. I know if I could start feeling part of the solution rather than part of the problem I'd feel a lot better.

A week later, Janine took a big risk, sharing that journal entry with the class. Subsequently, she wrote:

It was scary to do. But the big, wonderful thing was that at dinner June came to me and said she understood and wanted to give me a hug. That she at times felt it wasn't safe also. We had such a warm talk and others joined in. What a gift. It was worth the agony of saying what I had said.

Another important step occurs when Whites begin to replace their attempts at being colorblind with acknowledgment of racial background as part of a person's total identity. For example, in Judy's first journal entry she had noted: "I never think of race. One of my friends is Black, but I never think of her as Black. She's just a neat person." After a few classes, however, she reported telling her friend she now realizes that she is Black, and her friend responded, "I thought you would never notice."

Janet spells out evolving awareness of her issues in developing a friendship with a Black classmate; her writing also reveals that she is still engaged in that process:

When I first started the class, I thought I'd like to become friends with a Black person or a Chicano simply because they were people of color and it would be interesting to get to know someone different than myself. As time went on and we explored our life stories and different feelings, I started seeing my classmates of color as people similar to me and yet different, but all struggling with various problems. I found myself drawn to Candy. On the night she told about her daughter's problems in her school, I felt an inner rage at the inequality in our society. I was really surprised at my reaction because, though I've experienced rage before, it was only when the problems directly applied to me and my loved ones. She and I also share another class together. Our conversations began about our classes, but they took more personal direction.

Our friendship is developing. As this occurs, I find myself not noticing her color as much, but then this concerns me as I don't want to fall into the old pattern of pretending there are no differences. I don't want to develop this friendship based on Candy's Blackness, but on the fact we have a lot in common and enjoy talking with one another. At the same time, I'd like to learn about her growth as a Black woman, as I'm interested in all aspects of her. However, selfishly I also feel like I can learn something about my own racism by learning about her. I don't think this is too terrible to want this for me, as in any relationship I develop, there are areas I hope to enhance in myself. Maybe a true friendship with someone of color will be the recognition that there are differences in us, but if it is a friendship based on genuine feeling, then our similarities will be the primary focus of the relationship.

In sum, during this phase of growth, old attitudes and behavior toward people of color are reevaluated. Mistaken notions are discarded, and are gradually replaced by insights that contribute to the building of new relationships.

When the White students accept doing the hard emotional as well as cognitive work of uncovering and acknowledging their participation in racism, they take the crucial steps that bring them to the next phase of the journey to anti-racist consciousness and behavior. As Frank declared, looking back on his conflicts of this period: "I think the clue to my success was being willing to give up my image and go for broke. It bothered me to share my confusion and misunderstanding, but I valued my own growth more."

CONCLUSIONS

During this phase, all of the students experience a heightened awareness of the contradictions in their personal lives and in the practices of the institutions of society. They use the conceptual framework presented in this phase to examine these, and struggle to resolve the immensely powerful feelings aroused by their new insights.

Students can get stuck in these feelings, and thus the instructional pedagogy must guide the dynamics with care. However, while as co-teachers we create an environment in which people feel safe to take risks, safety must not be confused with comfort. It will be uncomfortable at times for everyone. But we do not allow students to use discomfort as an excuse for avoiding difficult issues. We provide gentle yet firm support to help students work through their discomfort and turmoil and establish the basis for personal growth.

The next chapter describes what happens when students do move on to the next major phase of their anti-racism journey.

CHAPTER 5

The Third Phase: Transformation to an Understanding of Self and Society

"You made my life less comfortable, and you enriched it. Along with painful truths, you gave each student the gift of your belief in them as a person who can make change happen," a student wrote to us at the end of one semester, aptly capturing the primary pedagogical task of the transformation period.

TEACHING CHALLENGES

Guiding students' learning of the specific knowledge and behavioral skills required to act effectively as anti-racists in their field of work becomes the focus of class sessions during this period. Our challenge is to spur students to take the necessary steps for growth, while avoiding the pitfalls—such as staying stuck in the emotions of the disequilibrium generated by the prior phase.

Teaching now reaps the rewards of earlier hard work. Sometimes we feel as if we are holding our breath until this period and then heave a big sigh of relief. Now we can breathe normally again. Teaching is more relaxed. The sessions become more fun, with humor and laughter. There is much energy for learning new information, solving problems, and trying out new behaviors.

Students take on more responsibility for supporting and challenging each other. They now have a sense of each other's strengths and weaknesses and are less anxious about how they look to their classmates and are consequently more open and honest, able to listen carefully to each other, and comfortable about engaging in critical dialogue. In fact, the class increasingly functions as a support group to which students bring their attempts to confront racism in their personal and work lives. Now the request "Help me figure out what to do" is appropriate.

However, while this is the overall picture, students in fact show considerable individual differences in the timing, intensity, and duration of the transitional period of disequilibrium and movement into the transformation phase. By the middle of the course, a few still cling to their first-phase denials of racism. Others are still grappling with the many emotions of the disequilibrium phase. Indeed, some never reach the third phase during the class, although students in this group do sometimes reach that destination after the course is over.

During the third phase, we conduct a "How are you feeling so far?" session (see Week 6, Activity 2). Always very moving, this activity not only gives students an opportunity for emotional release, but it also enables them to gain a new perspective on their turmoil, which each student usually had hitherto thought unique to him- or herself. The collective impact of their classmates' revelations places their individual struggles in a social context based on the larger issues of socialization in a racist society. This session is the turning point for many when "psychological defensiveness is replaced by effective and cognitive openness which allows the person to begin to be more critical in his/her analysis" (Cross, 1991, p. 85).

The ground rule regarding critical feedback among students now changes. Students are building ties with each other and with the teachers, and both should move to more open critical interactions. Accordingly, we allow significant disagreements between students to take their course, with facilitation by us as needed. Although these may produce anger, tears, and general discomfort at first, productive facilitating of the discussion both between students and among the whole group leads to impressive learning and usually to a higher level of trust that results from reconciliation.

Reading students' journals at mid-semester is a useful way to learn about individual problems and possible danger spots and to provide individualized responses. To a student stuck in ambivalence, "frustrated and scared to go farther," we wrote:

> Dear R: I think you are at one of those points of disequilibrium which is very uncomfortable and which will either resolve by moving into a new stage—in this case being anti-racist not just thinking about it, or resolve by going back to where you were before you took the course. Of course, you can also stay at the point of disequilibrium for a while; it may be safer than taking the leap forward and less guilt-ridden than taking a leap backward. Keep working on it. Try to write about why you are afraid to go farther. What do you think will happen to you? What are you afraid of losing?

To a student who had made impressive growth in the first part of the semester, but was overly critical of her progress, we wrote:

> Dear M: We are impressed with your progress in this class. So much good thinking and deep feeling. We know the feelings of being overwhelmed, having stomach aches, etc., are hard, and yet they are indicators of how much you care. We are also glad that you are feeling angry, a more energizing emotion. Of course you can't learn it all in a semester, but you have already accomplished the first important step, exposing the lies. Now

you can take the next one, gaining the information and skills to involve yourself in actual struggle in your way. It is clear, as you yourself are aware, that you are at a crossroads. Feel good about what you have accomplished, and keep your need to continue growing alive. Finding the time to do social activism work is possible, even in a busy schedule. Better to live with a certain amount of creative tension than to be numb. We know that you can do it.

In reply this student wrote: "Felt good reading your notes. I appreciated being validated." This comment highlights how important it is for us to remember to validate the steps each student takes. The notion of small changes is useful to keep in mind. Finally, the growth we see in our students also validates us. When our students assert "I will never view the world in the same way," we know we are accomplishing what we set out to do.

ACTIVITIES

Weeks 6 through 12 establish the main content of new information that we want students to use in learning how to think and operate as anti-racists. We design activities to give them the courage to step out of the past and into the present, freeing themselves to operate in new ways in the future.

There are many options for content and activities during these weeks, depending on the key dynamics and current issues when we are teaching the course, the backgrounds of students, and their work settings. We return to this point in Chapter 7.

Week 6: Taking Stock

This is a pivotal week. Its primary purpose is to provide an outlet for the tensions that have been building up in students and to help them gain deeper, collective insight into their feelings and the process of constructing anti-racist consciousness and behavior.

Activity 1: Children and Racism. This one-hour activity begins with a brief review of the assigned article followed by a concrete exercise. We teachers bring a collection of children's books to class, enough for one for each student. We select a range of problematic books using the following guidelines:

- Classics, Caldecott winners, popular current books
- Books with obvious stereotypes about an ethnic group
- Books that reflect omission (could have included illustrations of children/adults of color but did not)

- Books that demean an ethnic group—for example, through illustrations of animals dressed up as a member of an ethnic group (e.g., as a Native American) or with animals as stand-ins for people in stories/illustrations that reflect colonial or racist relationships
- Books that reflect a racist balance of power—for example, plots where the White children are the active ones and the children of color passive, or where White children are the leaders or rescuers of children of color

We also include some books that authentically and respectfully depict people from specific groups of color, or depict equitable relationships among an interracial/intercultural group of children/adults. For further ideas about children's books and racism, see Ramsey (1987), Derman-Sparks et al. (1989), and Kendall (1995).

Students break into small groups of three or four to critique children's books from the collection we have brought, evaluating how different racial/ethnic groups are portrayed through the story line, illustrations, and characterization. Each student chooses one book, looks it over, and then critiques it to her or his small group. Then the class discusses these questions:

- What feelings came up for you in the small-group discussion?
- What shall we do about books with racist messages?

We help students explore the issues raised by asking additional questions:

- Do we continue to share these books with our children and grandchildren?
- Do we give up using a particular book, or do we share it and discuss the racist messages with children?

Our teaching strategy for this activity is to involve all class members in the discussion and demonstrate the full panorama of feelings, issues, and obstacles that individuals encounter. The topic evokes strong feelings and disagreements because it raises one main contradiction that students are experiencing—how to change society, but do it without causing anyone discomfort. We do not expect the discussion to lead to closure or consensus. Rather, we emphasize the complexities, dilemmas, and emotions generated by the topic. Key pointers for this activity are as follows:

1. All students get an equal turn to speak in the small groups.
2. In the whole-group discussion, everyone has a right to his or her point of view.
3. Do not let a few students dominate; give everyone who wants to a chance to speak once before people have a chance to speak again.

Activity 2: How Are You Feeling So Far? By the sixth week, students need the opportunity to express their accumulating tensions collectively. The objectives of this activity (approximately 1 hour and 40 minutes) are to (1) enable students to hear each other ventilate feelings, (2) help them gain insight into why they are experiencing such emotions, and (3) facilitate movement to the next phase of growth. Either by going around in a circle or letting students choose turns, we ask each student to share with the whole class what they are feeling because of the course. Each person has two minutes. No questions are permitted and no comments allowed until everyone has had a turn. After these disclosures, we help the class identify key themes or patterns that emerge from the remarks.

Our teaching strategy for this activity is to help students acknowledge the feelings expressed and to learn from them. Most express considerable turmoil—describing feelings of guilt, shame, ambivalence, anger, and frustration as their old attitudes and understandings about racism and individual identity have been challenged by new perspectives and insights. During the discussion that follows, we—

1. Reassure students that each semester other students have expressed similar feelings
2. Look at the patterns and themes that have emerged and help students understand how these are connected to the realities of being socialized into either the oppressor or oppressed groups in this society
3. Ask White students to consider how their guilt is helpful neither to them nor to the struggle to eliminate racism
4. Ask students of color to consider their anger as a righteous and even inevitable response to the realities of racism—which needs to be directed toward specific targets for change, rather than turned inward or directed outward as unspecified frustration with and resentment against Whites in general
5. Suggest that, while the past cannot be changed, the present and future can and that beyond guilt, frustration, and anger lies action

Thus we raise a challenge to the whole group; "What are you going to do now?" We quote from Frederick Douglass to reinforce our point:

> Let me give you a word on the philosophy of reform. . . . If there is no struggle there is no progress. Those who profess to favor freedom, and yet deprecate agitation, are men [and women] who want crops without plowing up the ground. They want rain without thunder and lightening. They want the ocean without its many waters. This struggle may be a moral one; or it may be a physical one; or it may be both moral and physical; but it must be a struggle. (quoted in Foner, 1945, p. 61)

This session becomes a turning point as students discover that their turmoil is not only a symptom of their own problems but a collective response. They gain confidence from the knowledge that others have resolved these feelings, and we expect that they will too. Their awareness of each other deepens, and they are more understanding of how different people experience learning about racism. This shift provides a richer and safer context for interaction.

Week 7: Sexism, Classism, and Racism

Now that the class has established a conceptual framework about racism, we examine gender and class as additional contexts for institutionalized inequities, as well as the interrelationships between sexism, classism, and racism. Since a whole semester could easily be devoted to this topic, our purpose is only to introduce it as a supplement to the work on racism.

Activity 1: Class Identity Groups. In preparation for this 1-hour activity, students complete the reading assignment and write 2- to 3-page papers describing their socioeconomic identity (both for their family of origin and now) and their memories of how they learned about their class position. Students meet in small groups according to how they identified their class background (30 minutes) and share stories and ideas from their papers. Each group then decides and records on easel paper what that group wants to share with the whole class.

We reconvene the class, and each group has 5 minutes to report. We then identify key themes. If time permits, or as an alternative, we also use a "fishbowl" exercise. Here students of working-class background sit together in a circle in front of the class to talk about their sense of identity, the prejudices they feel others direct toward them, and what they want others to know about being members of this class. This equips both them and the rest of the group to deepen their understanding of the psychological impact of class inequality.

Activity 2: *Salt of the Earth.* Students watch the film *Salt of the Earth* (Jarrico & Biberman, 1951), a nonfiction account of a union struggle of Mexican American and European American miners to gain better working and living conditions. As they work together through a long and difficult strike, the changes in the relationship between the White and Mexican Americans and between the men and the women illustrates the impact of racism, sexism, and classism on people's lives and how these three "isms" interact.

Besides providing popcorn, our teaching strategy is to lead a brief postviewing discussion about student reactions to the film. Usually, we find that it offers students a strong positive message about the possibilities of challenging oppression.

Week 8: Moving into Action

Two activities during this session support students in (1) moving forward on their action projects, an important component of effectively carrying out new practices in their work, and (2) exploring their cultural identity more deeply.

Activity 1: Action Project Support Groups. Students meet for 1 hour in their support groups to report on the progress of their action projects. The support groups offer help with the difficulties students are encountering, additional ideas for strategies, and reinforcement for what they have already accomplished. Some have not yet begun their work; others are well into their projects. The encouragement of peers and the opportunity to talk about obstacles they have encountered and fears they are experiencing contribute to stimulating further progress, as do the examples provided by students who have already begun their work. By circulating among the groups, instructors also gain a good sense of which students need further individual support and which students are well on their way.

Activity 2: Exploring Cultural Identity. Students meet in "identity" groups for 1 hour to continue exploring the relationship among ethnicity, racism, and cultural issues and to deepen their understanding of their social role. Depending on the makeup of the class, small groups are formed in various ways: students of color, specific ethnic groups of color (e.g., African American, Latino, Asian American, and so forth), mixed (interracial/intercultural) students, Jewish students, Christian White students. The focus of discussion also varies:

1. *Students of color* continue to explore the changes in their feelings about their extended group identity and examine stereotyped attitudes between groups of color that interfere with communication and coalitions.
2. *Jewish students* explore the complexities of being White and Jewish in a society that gives them White privilege and at the same time is anti-Semitic. The discussion will sort through the confusion about their ambiguous, dual role as members of the dominant group on the one hand and members of a dominated group, on the other.
3. *Christian White students* explore cultural aspects of their specific ethnic identity and their feelings about being members of the dominant group.

In the last 10 minutes, each group chooses what issues they want to bring to the whole class. The whole class reconvenes, and each group has 5 minutes for its report.

Regarding teaching strategies, each small group does its own facilitating. The rule is that they agree on how to divide their time so everyone has a chance to speak before group discussion. We circulate in case there are questions and intervene if a group gets stuck or wanders off the subject. During the report back to the entire class, we ask students to listen respectfully to each other and wait until all groups are finished to ask clarification questions.

Week 9: Culture, Values, and Behavior

In this session we turn to a focus on culture rather than race. Activities provide information and experiences that (1) deepen students' understanding of cultural differences, (2) develop their ability to interpret behavior in a cultural context, and (3) stimulate thinking about how to improve the capacity of human service programs to reach culturally diverse populations. The principal objective of this session is to provide a more systematic way for students to continue their own study about different cultures. We do not expect to teach them all there is to know about a particular group, which of course would be impossible in the time available, but hope to give them some cognitive and attitudinal tools for continued learning on their own.

Activity 1: The "BaFá BaFá." In this activity, which requires 1 hour and 30 minutes, students role-play learning about a society very different from their own and attempt to interact on the basis of a new set of cultural rules. The instructions for this game, BaFá BaFá, are as follows:

1. Divide students into two cultures—Alpha and Beta. Each group reads about the values, expectations, and customs of its own new culture: Alphas are relaxed and value personal contact and intimacy within a sexist and patriarchal structure, while Betas measure a person's value by how well she or he performs in the marketplace.
2. Once the members of each group are comfortable with their new culture, observers are exchanged, and they attempt to learn the other culture by observing its members for a fixed period of time.
3. Observers return to their own culture and report what they saw.
4. Each group tries to develop hypotheses about the most effective way to interact with the other culture, and then sends a visitor who attempts to "live in" and adapt to the other culture. When everyone has had a chance to visit, the game ends. (*BaFá BaFá*, 1977)

A whole-class discussion follows, exploring feelings that arose during this experience. We then relate what students felt to the experiences culturally different children and adults have when they must learn the culture of the school or agency where our students work.

Activity 2: An Anthropologic Framework for Thinking About Culture.
After the experiential exercise, a lecture, based on a schema developed by Kluckhohn and Strodbeck (1961), offers an anthropological framework for defining culture, comparing cultural values and orientations, and interpreting behavior within different cultures. Kluckhohn and Strodbeck (1961) argue that five basic questions are addressed by every society:

1. What is the character of innate human nature? ("human nature orientation")

2. What is the relation of human beings to nature—and to the supernatural? ("man-nature orientation")
3. What is the temporal focus of human life? ("time orientation")
4. What is the modality of human activity? ("activity orientation")
5. What is the modality of human beings' relationship to one another? ("relational orientation").

In exploring this anthropological framework, we explain and use a table developed by Kluckhohn and Strodbeck (see Figure 5.1).

For a teaching strategy, we emphasize how the priorities and goals of various cultures are ordered in different ways, even though responding to the same basic human issues. We challenge students to envision the characteristics of a pluralistic society in which no one culture becomes the dominant system but in which varieties of cultures can coexist. Then we ask how human service programs would look in the context of such a pluralistic society, leading the class through an examination of biculturalism within the context of this framework. We ask: What are the difficulties and the strengths of being bicultural? What would be the strategy for effective education and other human service programs in such a society?

Often, the major attitudinal issue that arises in response to this session is students' defensiveness about their own culture and their need to have one right way

Orientation	Range of Variations		
Human nature	Evil *(mutable or immutable)*	Neutral or Mixture *(mutable or immutable)*	Good *(mutable or immutable)*
Man-nature	Subjugation to nature	Harmony with nature	Mastery over nature
Time	Past	Present	Future
Activity	Being	Being-in-becoming	Doing
Relational	Lineality	Collaterality	Individualism

FIGURE 5.1. The Five Value Orientations and the Range of Variations Postulated for Each. Adapted from F. Kluckhohn & F. Strodbeck, *Variations in Value Orientation* (New York: Row, Peterson, 1961), pp. 11–12.

for people to behave. We help them explore why the defensiveness arises and why the idea of multiple cultural approaches is threatening to them. We raise the point that racism teaches members of the oppressor or dominant group to fear anything but a monocultural approach to life.

Week 10: Culture, Values, and Behavior Continued

This class continues to examine issues of culture. One part focuses on cultural groups in the United States, the second on the imposition of European American values on cultures outside the United States.

Activity 1: Learning About Cultures. Students of the same cultural group meet and discuss the following questions:

1. What do you want others to know about your culture?
2. What are its key underlying rules?
3. What do you never want to hear others say about your culture?
4. How do you want others to learn about your culture?

This activity develops an awareness of the difficulties involved in deciding what to select from the myriad customs, beliefs, and behaviors of the culture and in agreeing on the critical patterns of one group. It also provides another look at the impact of racism and racial stereotyping on culture. Individual differences within a group emerge, based on specific, concrete experiences, and students must decide how to handle their differing perspectives. When the whole class reconvenes, discussion revolves around the issues they faced in making decisions about what to share with the class.

When the class composition is not sufficiently diverse to permit small-group meetings based on cultural similarities, we conduct an alternative activity: Students choose a specific cultural group to read about before the class session and then meet in small groups with classmates who have chosen the same cultural group to share what they have learned. (Using the excellent collection of books and periodicals at our campus library, students pursue reading assignments about Native Americans, Chicanos, African Americans, and others.) The following questions are guides for the small-group discussions:

1. What are some critical social, economic, and political issues for the group you read about? How did these issues affect the lives of the specific people you read about?
2. What are the significant elements in their cultural view? How did the particular people you read about articulate or demonstrate this?

3. How do the critical issues and cultural view differ from a White, European American one? How do they differ from your specific cultural view and sociopolitical realities? What are the conflicts? What are the similarities?
4. How do people experience racism, and what coping methods do they use?
5. How are the socialization and other life experiences of the people you read about concretely different from or the same as your own?

The instructors circulate during the small-group discussions, listening, asking probing questions, and keeping students on track. The instructors do not expect the small-group discussions to produce experts about a particular culture, but rather to sensitize students to the complexities of this task. When the large group reconvenes, each group reports about the major themes and issues explored, and we review the strengths and weaknesses of various techniques for continuing to learn about particular cultural groups.

Activity 2: Examining the Impact of Racism on Cultures Beyond the United States. Our objective is to expand students' recognition of the forms racism takes and to raise their awareness of its impact beyond our geographic borders. We use a video to introduce information on this topic, rather than readings or lecture, because this medium affects people both cognitively and emotionally, helping them to gain a sense of perspectives different from their own. There are several videos that serve the purpose of this session. A recent one is *Columbus Didn't Discover Us* (Echevarria, Van Lennep, Rivera, & Leppzer, 1992).

Concerning our teaching approach, we seek to enable our students to decenter themselves so that they gain an understanding that both historic and current events can be interpreted quite differently, depending on one's cultural perspective. The so-called triumph for Columbus and Europe, for example, was a saga of misery for the indigenous cultures of the Americas.

Week 11: Cultural Diversity, Racism, and Education

Deepening understanding of "culturally relevant" approaches to education and barriers to their implementation is the focus of this session. In different semesters we have focused on IQ, learning styles and curriculum, open education and multiculturalism, and bilingual education. Since cultural influences on learning styles and IQ are the most frequent topics, we describe these in more detail.

Activity 1: Culture and Learning Styles. We present a lecture about the origin and development of the concept of culture and learning styles, defining the terms used by people working in this field and summarizing the research about cultural influences on learning styles and its implications for teaching and evaluation. We also illustrate how behavioral racism is practiced in education by reviewing the work of researchers who find that present public school pedagogy favors children who have an analytic or field-independent learning style, which is more typical among middle- and upper-class European American children (Ramirez & Castaneda, 1974). Examining techniques for teaching children with alternative learning styles deepens our students' ability to work effectively with culturally diverse populations.

Students then meet in groups of three to talk about what they see are the characteristics of their learning style and how their school experiences as children and adults were a good or bad match. An alternative or supplementary activity is to show and discuss the video *Teaching Umoja* (Palmer & Cronin, 1996).

Activity 2: A Critique of IQ. A lecture with discussion centers on critiques of IQ, illuminating it as a tool for rationalizing institutional racist practices rather than as a valid concept for defining or measuring intelligence and children's ability to learn and think, particularly children of color (Gould, 1981, 1995; Guthrie, 1976; Kamin, 1974). Additional issues include the history of the development of IQ tests, particularly the Stanford Binet, the use made of IQ tests during different historical periods in the United States, court cases opposing their use and current status, and the revival of IQ testing in the 1990s. Discussion of IQ also provides an opportunity to discuss the interrelationship between educational methodology and racism.

Week 12: Alternative Adult Education Models

This session explores models for education and other human service work that can empower people who have been disenfranchised by institutionalized oppression. *Pedagogy of the Oppressed* (Freire, 1970) serves as the basis for this discussion. After a short review of the basic ideas in Freire's book, small groups examine the relevancy of his model to their own work. Each group shares its ideas with the class. We then discuss the principles and characteristics of leadership and professional-client relationships, which can help oppressed people in understanding their life experiences and enabling them to take control of their own lives. Students find the model suggested by Freire exciting because it offers concrete ideas and possibilities for developing human service work that can resist and transform the dehumanization that racism and other oppression inflict on our lives.

In some situations, we have considered using an alternative approach to this activity because students may find Freire's book hard going since it uses a new vocabulary, introduces new perspectives, and presents an unfamiliar analysis. One option is to have small groups of students read a chapter together before class and then report the key points in the chapter to the whole class. The instructor brings together these reports in an overview, and then the class goes to small groups to discuss the relevancy to their work.

STUDENT RESPONSES

A shift in students' response to the cognitive and emotional disequilibrium of the second phase ushers in this next phase of growth. Rather than feeling overwhelmed or stuck "in the mire," they now search actively for the knowledge and tools that will help them address the contradictions of a racist society in themselves and bring an anti-racist perspective to their work and community. This leads to transformations in their consciousness, attitudes, and behavior.

White Students

At the heart of White students' transformation is nondefensive acknowledgment of their participation in a racist society. The energy that once was consumed in defending and hiding their racism or feelings of guilt and inadequacy can now be applied to learning how to be anti-racists.

Barbara's summary of the steps to this point of her journey illustrates this process clearly:

> There was a definite process of change within me: From nervousness about hating what was exposed as my character to defensiveness. Then nothing for about two weeks. Then anger. I'm very tired of hearing about our pain. I think we are just going to have to accept it, experience it, and go about deciding what we are going to do about what is causing it for all of us— racism. After that, I began to come to terms with what I was and what I wanted. This class became actively interesting, not just as a class, but as a tool for my everyday life.

Martha more specifically describes the moment when she came to terms with herself:

> Okay, so I recognize my ethnocentrism and victim-blaming logic today. This evening was a turning point for me. Before, I was beginning to wonder if I really wanted to stay in this class and subject myself to many miserable feelings. I am so angry about my racism that I am determined to stay. I decided that I really want to learn and grow.

A week later she found that

I'm learning openly to discuss racially oriented topics without being so afraid that I will reveal my unconscious racism. Everybody knows it anyhow. Also, I thought I was secretly creepy for being White, but now I'm sure I'm not. It's just that I've got a lot to learn.

Ann describes her moment of critical change more succinctly:

The idea that we need to get off the pity pot was an eye-opener to me. The statement really got me thinking about what I was going to do.

Understanding Institutional Racism. Students begin to grasp the pervasiveness of racism and see its manifestations everywhere. Rachel's comment about her new critical eye echoes those of many others:

I've suddenly realized how critically observant I've become. In every commercial, every TV show, every newspaper article, I look for racist, classist, sexist attitudes, and underlying messages and I see them everywhere. I find myself wondering if things have gotten worse, or if I'm the one who has changed—and now I see what was always there.

Janet adds another aspect of White students' heightened awareness:

Whites still control the strings in all the places that really matter. Until Blacks, Latinos, Asians, and Native Americans participate proportionately represented in our boards of directors, executive levels, government policy making levels, and in stock ownership, the people of the Third World will remain essentially powerless to determine their future in this country.

The critique of victim-blaming, previously threatening to White students' self-image, now helps them put the puzzle together. As Frank explains:

I resisted reading *Blaming the Victim* [Ryan, 1976] because of its being labeled an exposé of middle-class ideology and me not feeling too great about being middle class anyway. But finally I dug in. It was a great feeling when you find a piece of a puzzle that has been eluding you for so very long. The concept of victim-blaming has changed the way I perceive countless situations now. It's a lens with which to see to the bottom of the classist, racist, sexist murk. It has transformed my perceptions of where responsibility truly lies. Moreover, it moved me out of the inaction of mea culpa to an understanding of behavior which can be changed.

As they begin to see racism everywhere, students are ready to accept even the most difficult concepts, like racism by omission. Amanda explains:

I think that I finally understand how Whites are either racist by commission or racist by omission because there is no middle ground. So you think by treating minorities equally and caring for friends and even having sexual and marriage ties with people of color that there is proof to the world and to yourself that you are not racist. Still, in your daily work the Whites get the best pay and the best jobs. In your school the education is geared for White culture, financial aid is allocated to White students primarily, and you notice it, perhaps, and think it should not be so, but you omit the action that tries to correct the injustice. I think the single belief that we are not racist because we are not doing racist actions overtly keeps us from seeing we are racist by omission.

Whites are ready to confront each other about racism, viewing these small acts as important in overturning racism. Julie describes how

in another class of mine a White student insisted she understands how hard it must be to be a minority, but she didn't know why everyone was making such a stink about the budget cuts to bilingual education. It wasn't until one of the Black students in class called her attitude racist that some of the White students, including me, said anything. We as Whites have gotten used to hearing a certain level of racism and don't stand up and scream at the injustice until it's too late. I or another White should have spoken out before the Black students had to.

Confronting Personal Racism and Responsibility for Change. Three interrelated developments occur in the way White students now deal with personal racism: (1) identifying nondefensively their own internal racist attitudes, (2) acknowledging their accountability for present-day racism, and (3) accepting responsibility to eliminate racism in the future. At precisely the moment students accept the inevitability of their own internalized racist attitudes as a consequence of an institutionally racist society, they feel empowered to decide what they will now do. Linda admits to herself:

The problem is that I have this racist voice in my head. When there is a Black woman swimming at the pool where I swim, it is the voice that says, "Where are your things, are they safe, because why else would she be here but to case the joint?" I keep swimming, shocked that it's still so bad. I know it's my mother's voice, the one that warned me of Black cleaning ladies, the ones from whom valuables must be hidden. But it saddens and distresses me that I still carry it.

What do I do with this voice? I acknowledge and counteract it with the reality I know to be different and go on? What else is there to do but to go on. It's easy for me to fall into thinking that I have such a racist upbringing that there is no hope. Every step of awareness is a struggle and requires that I work through the mush of feeling bad about myself and my family. However, I understand the need also to focus on positive feelings and aspects as well and that self-acceptance is prerequisite to the acceptance of others. Gradually I'm getting there.

Deepened self-comprehension and expanded appreciation of institutional racism facilitate a transformation of guilt and defensiveness into acceptance of responsibility for acting against racism. In this light, Beth explains that

what releases me to learn and act is my recognition that we are all racists because of institutional racism, and that it is not a question of atonement for the past. I can't change that. But, I can take action in the present. Before, I saw this as the work of others: those Whites who made prejudiced remarks or who wouldn't hire Blacks. They were the ones who had to change. Now I recognize that racism is so deeply ingrained in our society that the work to root it out is the work of all Whites because consciously or unconsciously, we all participate in keeping it alive. Knowing that the society is racist and breeds racism requires that I accept responsibility to aid others to realize the situation as it exists and to work at effecting change.

Moreover, students now feel energized to act. Ruth discusses how insights about the distinction between nonracism and anti-racism freed her to work with other Whites:

Once I began to see myself as a White person within a social structure, many of my previous misconceptions about being nonracist and my fears about confronting this issue with other Whites became much clearer to me. I realized that my own fear about having any racist attitudes was making it difficult for me to deal with people openly and effectively about racism. I was afraid to ask questions or assert my ideas for fear of exposing my own ignorance or racist attitudes. The obvious result of this is that I wasn't learning much and I wasn't teaching much, and I felt very insecure and afraid when confronted with this issue. My experience in the class has helped me realize that being an anti-racist is not founded on what racist attitudes a person doesn't have but rather is based on what anti-racist ideas, goals, and actions one takes part in to combat racism. So, for me this concept of anti-racist has been a very liberating one.

Facing the Psychological Dynamics of Whiteness and Cultural Identity. Ruth's exploration of the dynamics underlying a White classmate's discounting a Black classmate's anger illustrates another crucial element in her evolving anti-racist consciousness:

> Driving home after class, I tried to convince myself that I was overreacting to the incident. But the more it nagged at me with various chaotic thoughts and feelings, the more compelled I felt to write about it and try to understand exactly what it meant to me. Additionally, all I've learned this semester was saying to me that I had a responsibility to do so—minimizing it would only be opting for the least risky cop-out. It seems to me that a White cannot discount Black anger without being racist and without staking his own claim, however subconscious, in the substantial American heritage of racism.
>
> The basic message of the discount was "B is exaggerating and blowing things out of proportion." The discount therefore denies via trivialization that our Black classmate may indeed have something about which to be royally, righteously, and legitimately angry.
>
> Frankly, I don't think the root of your problem was trying to find out why B was angry (as you said it was), or you wouldn't have used loaded and downright insulting words to get your answers. Your problem, I think, was with admitting to the validity of her anger (even though you don't know its causes) and, more important, with even permitting her to be angry at all.
>
> I wonder, my White sister, what caused you not to have learned enough in this semester even to hesitate, to pause before you blurted out? Have you learned nothing of the subtle and powerful ways in which individuals (in this case, I think, you yourself) are affected and controlled by a history of racism? I ask you these questions as I ask myself.

Ann writes about another key insight after reading Albert Memmi's *The Colonizer and the Colonized* (1965):

> This book touched me most profoundly. I often recognized myself in his description of "the colonizer who refuses." The portrait of the individual enjoying the privileges of the colonizer yet horrified by the injustices of the colonized, believing that she wishes all people well and justifying herself with a position of principle—that was me.

As students struggle to understand the structural role of Whites in a systematically racist society, they also construct a more critical understanding of the human costs of racism to Whites. For example, Dan sets forth his new insights into the "psychology of the oppressor":

Reading Freire's *Pedagogy of the Oppressed* (1970) had an enormous impact on me. He does a brilliant job of explaining the psyche of the oppressor. He says that "the oppressors do not perceive their monopoly on having *more* as a privilege which dehumanizes others and themselves. They cannot see that, in their egoistic pursuit of having as a possessive class, they suffocate in their own possession and no longer are; they merely have" (p. 45). These insights helped me understand what I don't like in my own culture. I hope this will help me choose what I want to keep and what I want to change.

Amanda also reflects at length on her feelings about her culture:

The last few weeks I've been sifting so many things about what really matters to me, about what I need in my life, about what will bring me enjoyment and fulfillment. I find myself feeling so sad about the tragic contradictions in White culture. I have never wanted to be competitive. I remember feeling uneasy in high school when the heavy indoctrination began: to beat out your fellow students, to be better than everyone else. I hated the people that bought it and used it to split us all apart. And I kept being a sucker for trying to bring people together. Yet I learned a lot about friendship.

How did Whites ever get themselves so uptight and unnatural? What I'm realizing ever more is how much racism has made us the way we are. I just feel so sad about it. How do you change the course of culture from material to human feeling? How can I find the fulfillment I seek when I need other caring lives to work with, to care with? And those other people are going down the conveyor belt of propaganda, believing that we live for fame, money, and for our own self only, believing that relationships and friendships are only the reward at the end of the rainbow, instead of the daily bread that keeps us alive and human.

The process of weighing the strengths and limitations of their ethnic group culture and identity eventually has a very positive impact on White students' sense of self. Don explains:

It felt like I had this big closet to clean out, and I had taken everything out and was now trying to decide what stayed, what needed fixing, and what to throw out. It's a big job but it feels great. I know I am going to be more of the person I want to be.

Constructing Pluralistic Consciousness. Facing and coming to terms with the consciousness engendered by their structural role in racism opens the possibilities for constructing a truly pluralistic consciousness during this phase. One significant step is recognizing what it might be like for people of color to listen to Whites work through their racist attitudes, because earlier in the course so many were angry when they were not offered assurances of absolution. Ann, for example, relates that

> Carol said something tonight about overcoming parts of herself to be able to teach the class. I just about died. I realized I have never stopped to consider what it was like for her or for the other students of color to sit and listen to my personal racism. What a gamble it is, for no one can guarantee that in the end I will be able to overcome my upbringing and change. Carol is terribly supportive of me. I was really feeling down, and she came over to me after class and we talked about this. I asked her how people of color could possibly stomach the things they were hearing from Whites. She replied that what kept her going were the signs of the genuine work that White students were doing toward overcoming the attitudes and behaviors and that she didn't blame us so much as she blamed the system of racism into which we were forced.

Some deepen their awareness of what it means to be "in the minority" by temporarily experiencing it themselves. Allan found such an incident to be crucial for his further growth:

> Yesterday I attended a workshop given by Black educators. Many things crystallized for me. At times I felt very uncomfortable because I was one of the only Whites there. I did not at all feel uncomfortable with the people there; they were very accepting and very pleasant. But it was very important that I was in the minority because I don't know if half that information would have seeped in if I were feeling comfortable in a majority.

Judy contributes a similar experience:

> I went to the LA Cultural Center last night to see a play by a Black playwright. I don't know if I EVER put myself in an experience like that before where I'm one of the very few Whites among almost all Black people. For the first time I felt like the outsider as opposed to the insider part of the crowd. Somehow last night seemed like a really critical experience for me.

Grappling with the varied perspectives and knowledge generated by differential experiences in a racist society is yet another key step in the anti-racism journey. Janine writes:

> I asked myself what I can do about racism. I have learned to begin by accepting the limits of my own White understanding. I am learning that the need to see and appreciate that there is more here before me in this Black mother whose child I teach than I can ever fully understand. . . . I am learning to listen from my White limits and to your Black boundaries, and I can see that I have a responsibility for learning the ways in which my own racism and the racism of this country deny Blacks their boundary and their rights to set them.

As students let go of their old ways of thinking, they can engage in serious study about people of color without distorting the information. Reading, observing, and talking with others about different ways of life, values, and world views expands their ability to discern how cultures differ and interconnect. They can develop skill in interpreting behavior within the context of sociocultural reality, for they are now better able to practice a degree of humility vis-à-vis other ways of living. Rachel describes how her new consciousness led to changes at her yearly presentation to the predominately Black parents of her preschool:

> I have previously seen the meeting as an opportunity to talk about readiness skills and the types of things parents could do with their children at home to prepare them for the kindergarten curriculum. When I began to consider materials for this year's presentation, I realized that I could no longer do it the same way. Instead, I decided to make my belief known that many teachers offer less than quality education to Black children because they don't know how to meet their needs most effectively in the classroom. I also talked about how parents have the power, collectively, to help their children to receive a higher level of education by being involved with the school and with the teachers, and suggested some ideas for how this could be done.
>
> My presentation was well received. Several parents remained after to ask questions and share experiences. The reality of an institutionally racist system seemed to come as no great shock to them. My desire was to own that reality as a member of a majority culture and the need to confront the issue, and to support parents to do so also.

Another particularly powerful achievement is an understanding that relationships between Whites and people of color walk in a long shadow of history. Stunned by this insight, and wishing that it were not so, White students in this third phase recognize its reality:

> I feel that I finally understand the difference between the personal and the political, . . . and that causes me to feel like I grew up. On a personal level,

that is, I don't feel personally hurt if people of color need to do things separate from me. I realize this is the price I have to pay as a White for racism. Racism prescribes our relationships even when we are being anti-racist. This makes me very sad and angry and renews my determination to fight against the racism which is at the source of all of it.

In summary, new consciousness about racism and cultural differences opens the doors to establishing nonexploitative interracial relationships in the students' work and personal lives. When the difficulties are acknowledged and therefore have a chance of being worked through together, possibilities for meaningful and lasting ties increase. At first many report feeling self-conscious. Sometimes they apply new information about a group too broadly, because they forget to pay attention to the specific ways in which an individual lives his or her culture. Sometimes people are so anxious to be anti-racist that they are unable to see individuals in their complex wholeness. Gradually, however, for those who are willing to risk making mistakes and to learn from them, new relationships are possible—and very much worth the effort expended. Ultimately, understanding and acceptance of cultural differences enable students to get in touch with and share our essential, shared humanity.

Making Connections with Gender and Class. In the beginning of the course, some students invariably attempt to use experiences of class- or gender-based oppression as an excuse for not confronting their participation in racism. Now students' developing consciousness about racism improves their ability to explore how other forms of institutional oppression affect Whites, increasing their understanding of sexism and classism. An awareness of the interconnections strengthens their growth toward anti-racism. Although adequate study of these topics requires more than a few class discussions, even the limited time spent on these topics supports students' growth by giving sexism and classism a place to fit into the new puzzle, providing additional avenues for empathy and alliance between Whites and people of color. Christy explains the impact on her of making these connections:

Tonight I came to the realization regarding how sexism has played into my awareness of racism. It was like someone turned the light switch on. For the last few years I've known I've been discriminated against because I'm a woman and I've been living with rage about it. I wanted to be a doctor, not a nurse, but was pushed into doing the latter. My parents didn't even think a girl needed a college education; all I was good for was marriage. Tonight I realized I can use some of this inner rage to hook up with other minorities and their oppression. They are so closely interrelated for me that I'm surprised I didn't see it before. This awareness is really exciting because I had this hidden fear that some of my changes in the course were superficial and wouldn't stand up once the support of the class was gone, that I'd just drop back to the ethnocentric way I was. With this bridge, I've gathered more depth and understanding of myself and my attitudes and know that I'll never return to the same kind of person I was before the course. I love this new commitment to myself.

Often in unexpected places, students draw links between racism and sexism that deepen their understanding. Rachel writes about an experience like this at the theater:

At the end of the play the cast came out for a discussion with the audience composed mostly of White women. A White man spoke first, saying he thought it was good for women to see this play. It angered me, but I didn't know why. Later, discussing this incident with my friends, I went click-click-click, oh, yeah: blaming the victim. It was none of his business to worry about what women can get out of this play. His job should have been to see what he could get out of it as a White man. Nevertheless, he acted like sexism was a problem that women have, as if it's not a social problem for everyone, including him.

Martha describes a major breakthrough in her relationship with people of color because of seeing the film *Salt of the Earth* (Jarrico & Biberman, 1951), which explores the complex interplay between racism, sexism, and classism:

Last night I noticed a big change in myself. I'm feeling confused right now about the relationship of racism and sexism and I feel like I want to ask Kathy [a Black student] if she shares the feeling. Two weeks ago, I would have been scared shitless that she'd bite my head off. Now I don't think she will, but even if we do have disagreements or she confronts me about my racism or something, I know I can handle it.

My discussion with Kathy and the subsequent class discussion about the points of agreement and difference between Whites and women of color also helped me get yet another piece of the pie of how racism can influence us even when we are thinking we are fighting for the rights of all women, and how hard we have to work to make sure that the issues we choose are right for all women and not just for those of us who are White and middle class. Now I can look at the class as a practice ground to struggle with these issues together.

Some students find that their class socialization complicates their search for anti-racist consciousness; others can use their experiences as a bridge to understanding oppression. For example, Amanda, whose class origin is upper middle class, describes the complex set of emotions she feels about this aspect of her life:

I've been thinking about how growing up as wealthy and White "entitled" me to a whole range of experience and exposure which is both part of my background and who I am now. From birth on, I quickly learned that the world was made to work for me, learned about power, learned how to act so as to be accepted as one of the privileged. I learned my own private blend of arrogance and socialness, mixed with "appropriate" amounts of guilt and social concern . . . taking it as my God-given right that I should have much more than enough of everything. And then, you could be (and should be) "generous" and give a very little of your "more than enough" (though never enough that it hurt) to the "unfortunates" who had "not nearly enough." As different parts of my background surface, I feel a variety of things—the privilege of it all, but also embarrassment, anger, deep sadness, so much to unlearn.

In contrast, Steve, who grew up in a poor White working-class family in the South, developed a different sense of his personal identity and the relationships between his racial and class position. He states that "confusion and perplexity always surrounded racial identity for me," and then goes on to explain how:

Early in life I recognized that I was White, yet I and my family did not enjoy the fruits of the White community. In fact, I never remember feeling community at all. We were very poor. My father never received more than $3,500 a year, and we were a family of eleven. I envied Black people when I was a child. I thought they had a sense of community. They identified with each other and shared common bonds—a bond of color, of poverty, of class, even geography (the city I grew up in was very segregated). Whenever I observed Black people, I noticed they always waved and smiled and exchanged greetings with any other Blacks they met. To be Black meant you shared something with all other Blacks; you were family.
	It saddened me that color separated everything because I identified strongly with Blacks. They were poor like us. As I grew up, of course, I began to realize that no matter what my economic or social history was, where my family was from, or where we lived, I could always hide behind my whiteness, and I could even change my status within the White society. I might be on the bottom of the pile, but I was on the right pile. Black people did not have that option. They could not erase their skin.

Janine's struggle illustrates that of many of our students who felt caught between their past and present class background:

I grew up as a privileged member of the upper middle class, but in the last several years if one were to judge by my income, I probably would fit into the working-class category. In lots of ways I feel more comfortable around working-class people and share many of their beliefs. Yet, I don't share the same background or experiences or understanding as working-class people. So I'm left feeling lost, somewhere in the middle.

Some weeks later, Janine returned to this topic, describing how she found a way to resolve her conflict by constructing a new perspective about the meaning of being anti-racist:

Something really struck me in class tonight. In looking at sexism and racism, one could focus on a common oppression—the system—and so focus our rage in a more constructive direction. All of it was and is totally unjust; I would like to eliminate all forms of oppression. This idea, plus certain of Freire's concepts are opening new areas of understanding to me. I can never really know what it's like to be the victim of racism. Yet I can know what it's like to be the victim of sexism and I can relate what I know of one to the other . . . also to what Freire is talking about when he speaks of rebellion by the oppressed as a gift to the oppressor too, because it's an opportunity to get their humanity back.

Students of Color

Students of color, too, are trying out new ways to think about and interpret the problems they face. It is a process of redefining who they are by redefining what the history of their people has truly been. It is a search for new understanding about what underlies how others responded to them, as well as why they respond to other people as they do. The new information presented to them in class through lectures, readings, and discussions provides the context for reinterpreting their experiences.

As they seek ways to resolve the contradictions, students of color become acutely conscious of several facts, namely that (1) racism is a society-wide system rather than a series of loosely connected individual "mean people"; (2) the system of institutional racism is well-oiled and self-perpetuating, and will not change on its own; and (3) their fate as individuals is inextricably bound to the fate of their people. As they better understand the dynamics of institutional racism, their anger toward individual people now becomes anger toward the system. This shift demands new relationships with the world.

Constructing New Extended Group Identity. One observable shift occurs in the relationship between the students' self-concept and their beliefs about the ethnic/cultural base of their people. Once students of color understand that they have been co-opted into operating with false information about the history of their own people, they react against the internalized oppression that has forced them to remove themselves from strong group identity. They thus become consciously ethnocentric in situating their own identity within their group and in their pursuit of the truth about their people.

A consuming interest in reading about the experiences—historical and contemporary—of their own racial and ethnic group engages many. A Chicana student declares:

> Yesterday, I bought lots of books on Mexican American history and psychology, and I am very anxious to lay out a plan about where I go from here to learn about my Chicano race. I know that I will never be a rebel, but I am hoping for a full-fledged Chicana. I've become very excited.

An African American student vividly describes an awareness

> for the first time of the importance of my ethnicity and the awareness has electrified me to go on to all the areas of my life to see how my ethnicity relates to redefining them: my early home environment, my work environment, my relationships with my spiritual family at my Temple, my own inner environment. It feels like spring cleaning—with some articles (thoughts and attitudes) being completely discarded, some auctioned off or shared, and some just dusted off and better cared for.

Students decide to stop reacting to the way White society views their group and to begin searching for ways of acting in a culturally consistent framework. As one student put it, "You have to be what you damned are."

Carolyn is explicit about what new aspects of identity are going to replace previous ones:

> I'm especially sensitive to the feelings of resentment expressed by Mitsuye Yamada (1976) in her poem—about how people expect Asian women to be charming, entertaining, but not outgoing in ways that might threaten. Folks generally relate to me in this manner—ignoring the things I've said because they don't fit the image they have of me: mediator, all understanding, quiet/sympathetic. I thoroughly enjoyed and am going to take up Mitsuye's entreaty—that what each of us needs to do about what we don't know is to go look at it. I am beginning to put the issues of my ethnicity in order.

Much power comes with the reclaiming and reconstructing of identity, as if students now release the energy that they previously had used to defend against feeling inferior. Theresa describes this when she writes that

I used to think being Mexican was something to be ashamed of—something dirty and dumb. I gradually shed that. However, there were often times I could not feel safe in expressing my feelings. It often took some effort to defend my right to be what I am, especially when circumstances seemed hostile, when those present were obviously racist. It still hurts to be looked at askance, but now I'm not afraid of facing MY feeling as though I'm less than anyone. I don't buy it anymore. I'll shout my ethnicity to anyone.

This struggle to know who one is in relation to one's cultural group also expresses itself in the strong need at this time for cultural and/or racial homogeneity—to be around others of one's own group. The journey is reflected through such comments as the following:

I love the time spent with other Black women—just hanging out. It gives me space to be selfishly nice to myself and not always eating/digesting other people's garbage.

I wish I could find some comrades like myself who are coming out of their shell—beginners. I find it difficult to relate to Chicanos who talk over my head.

I have enough to learn about myself—there just isn't enough time to learn about the rest of the world.

Creating New Relationships with People of Color and Whites. As students identify the specific context in which they can best nurture their own growth and take time to get what they need, they also become more open to building new kinds of relationships with other people of color. Student writing reveals that the common experience of oppression is a strong bond:

What a supportive and uplifting experience I had in class talking with other students of color. We were openly saying how White people bothered us. It feels so good to examine the things we had grown up believing about Whites, how we had tried to emulate them, and now how we are so much stronger because we know the truth. Why are we imitating a group that has so much to learn about human interaction, when it is clear that Third World people of color possess a distinct strength in people-to-people relations? We have so much to learn to value about ourselves and to teach our children.

Further, understanding that the common experience of oppression stems from the same source—institutional racism—helps students of color overcome negative feelings about members of other racial groups. As one Black student writes, discussing her prejudices toward Mexicans:

> A great deal of difference exists, I'm learning, between personal prejudice and racism that results from political oppressions against a group of people. I enjoyed discovering that I was not a racist monster after all, and that the unfortunate result of oppression is the creation of a chain of prejudices as a reaction rather than an action in itself. Reading gave me some concrete information about Chicano culture and problems with which they are dealing. Their fight is so identical to the Black one!

Now, students of color are able both to hold on to the notion that they are embedded in a particular group with a particular history that makes them different from members of other groups and to see where commonalties lie. They are more comfortable talking openly about intergroup differences without feeling the pressure for hierarchical comparisons. They now see their oppressive experiences as qualitatively different rather than solely in degrees of severity.

Along with the students' deepening understanding of the meaning of their own ethnicity comes a new perspective on the negative impact of racism on White human development and the world as a whole. This perspective does not constitute a reason to forgive or even excuse Whites for their racism, but it allows for a reinterpretation of what students of color had previously believed to be the experience of Whites. Marita, who was intensely interested in helping White professionals understand Hispanic culture, relates how this new understanding helped her deal with a challenging situation:

> One session which I was leading was very frustrating. A White psychiatrist who attended continuously questioned my statements which felt to me like she was attempting to invalidate me. She would always want to bring up other issues which were not relevant at the time, and I finally told her that the purpose of the session was to deal with Hispanic issues and nothing more. I explained to her that I understood that individuals had many dimensions to their personalities, but we were here to discuss cultural issues, an area that many professionals don't understand when working with clients because their training totally ignores it. She quieted down.
>
> I realized that, for White staff, dealing with individual problems of Hispanic clients is comfortable, but when racism is the topic, they become very quiet and say very little. They obviously have difficulty accepting or admitting any racist attitude in themselves. This is something that I understand, but I can't absolve them from being racists. I know they simply absorbed what is in society—without even trying. Though this situation makes me mad as hell, it's not them I'm angry at any more.

New perspectives on the reality of being White also make some students more questioning of previously accepted or unexamined behavior, as Yvette comments:

> I'm not saying that I don't respect the people in this class for the pain they've subjected themselves to, because I have seen them sweat, but I can't think of one good reason Whites would want to change a society where they reap all the benefits. It really makes me wonder about the Whites I know who SAY they hate racism and want the society to change—I wonder if they're talking about the same kind of change I'm talking about?

Michael succinctly sums up the changes in thinking about Whites that happen during phase three. "I've been around White folks all my life and yet it's only now that I see where I need to unhook from some of the images I have both of them and of myself."

Reexamining One's Role in Social Change. Students of color also struggle to make a match between their new consciousness about institutional racism and their own activity in a collective sphere. They can no longer be satisfied with being frustrated and angry at "all White people." They test out new strategies for more proactive engagement.

Carmen reveals the beginning of a more active role and her still-unresolved conflicts about the value of so doing:

> I sat next to a cop at a diner. Hearing him talk about the tactics they use when approaching Chicanos or Blacks made me cringe. I suggested that when he was harassing a victim simply walking across a parking lot that the person might be innocently walking home from work. He said, "They don't work." His self-righteous, better-than-thou attitude was so upsetting that I wanted to throw something at him. But the circumstances did not warrant my even raising my voice. People like that have a lot invested in keeping things as they are. Well, I know there are economical, political, and psychological reasons for bigotry and racism to exist. Just as I know there are ways to eliminate them. Not quickly of course, but in time—I have high hopes, and I'm going to be a part of making it happen.

Helen's writing demonstrates her awareness that the only way to maintain one's cultural integrity while operating in a society dominated by a notion of White superiority is to work on ways to change the oppressive nature of that society:

> It's clear that the inequities of the system will exist for another generation at least. But one method that can be used to overcome many issues is to

acquire an "open mind" so that we may see our realities and alternatives. These are the questions that we need to ask ourselves: (1) Who are we? (2) Where do we find ourselves? (3) Where are we going? (4) What are we leaving the next generation? Then we need to establish groups of all ages and begin an in-depth study together about our history, culture, economics, migration patterns, and the Independence Movement to find answers. Our next step would be to urge all concerned to make a commitment to their community by working collectively so that everyone could pull out of the quagmire together instead of opting for the individualistic approach where only a few succeed.

At the same time, students also struggle with the contradictions between the power of institutional racism and the possibilities for change. Nevertheless, even with the uncertainty, students feel compelled to do something:

The more I read books like *Even the Rat Was White* (Guthrie, 1976), the more I feel the bigness of it all. Man, I can't believe how calculated the efforts have been to keep people of color at the bottom! It's a conspiracy! It almost makes you feel that if you want to do anything it's like trying to take on the U.S. army with a water pistol. . . . But then I think about my alternative—being complacent and doing nothing. That's just what they want me to do—nothing. I can't live with that either. I have to do SOMETHING.

They also speculate about the different routes for change:

What I have got into perspective for myself by being in this class is that there's a difference between trying to change something from the inside and trying to change it from without. In most of our discussions in this class, we define it as work from the inside. This is because I feel that the people in our class don't quite believe that the society we live in has to be thrown out. They think it can be modified. More critical than this, I believe that as a class, some of us who see a goal of integration or pluralism are on one end; some of us who are not sure what will work are in the middle; and some of us who are for separation and race nationalism are on the other end. The two ends oppose one another and therefore I don't see us as really getting into a collective perspective on social change. When I engage in dialogues like I did with this class, it brings me closer to understanding that I have to decide which end I'm on. I don't want to sound negative, but right now I don't think that any modification or "inside" changes will really work.

In summary, the reexamination of their extended group identity and a deeper understanding of institutional racism lead students of color to reexamine relationships with other people of color and Whites, as well as to a new sense of their commitment to act in the face of racial injustice. In the Freirean sense (Freire, 1970), each becomes the Subject of action versus the Object of someone else's action. Jose illustrates this process:

> Today I felt immersed in power. My identity has been returned to me, and I have reflected and thought about the injustices that racism has dealt me and will continue to deal my people. Being angry and sad is of little use. The power that I've regained must be put to use. I promise myself that I shall be ready and aware of racism. I know that this is an unending process that will grow and mature, but never end.

Barbara's last journal entry is a fitting final comment:

> This course was most important to me because after many years of struggling with self-acceptance physically and ethnically, I am finally able to do so. Also, it has raised my consciousness and made me aware that one cannot become complacent, REGARDLESS OF YOUR AGE, but must always be working with others to carry out strategies for change so that this society will become fair to all.

CONCLUSIONS

The transformations that begin to occur in the third phase reveal both significant similarities and differences between Whites and students of color, reflecting the impact of being on either side of racism's power divide. In general, students of color move toward—

1. *Reclaiming and affirming their extended group identity, and therefore themselves.* New identity is based on their own group's definition of themselves, not that of the dominant society.
2. *Constructing a frame of reference.* Students locate responsibility for the creation and evolution of racism in the institutions of the dominant society.
3. *Building new relationships.* They can now develop relationships with other people of color and with Whites.

White students move toward—

1. *Constructing a new extended group identity.* They can discard the false notions of nonracism while seeking to keep what is good and abolish what is bad in European American culture.
2. *Developing a critical understanding of racism.* They can critique institutional structures and accept responsibility of racism as a White problem.
3. *Building real relationships.* They can consciously establish more equitable relationships with people of color.

For all students, we hope the last phase of their journey is moving to active engagement in individual and collective anti-racist acts. As one student aptly remarked, "Anti-racist training is confrontation with self and then going out and affecting the world." Chapter 6 describes these next steps.

CHAPTER 6

The Fourth Phase: Anti-Racism as a New Beginning

Believing in the importance of social and personal change is one thing. Doing it is another. Ultimately, anti-racism depends on acting on the belief that personal and social change is possible. Unless students act on their perceptions of themselves as having the ability and the power to impact systems, new knowledge and attitudes are meaningless. The underlying goal of anti-racism education is for individuals to become self-motivated activists, able to apply their new consciousness to work behavior and personal life.

TEACHING CHALLENGES

The action-project requirement is pivotal to our model of anti-racism education—insisting that students take action to change something. It is the testing ground on which students publicly take a stand and, so to speak, put their money where their mouths are. Meeting this requirement does not come easily. Nevertheless, the experience of doing it both contributes to students' increased understanding of how racism operates and enhances their feelings of self-esteem and power.

We learned from the mistakes we made the first few times we taught the course (when up to 50% of the class might not complete the social action requirement) that it is very important to provide ongoing support structures from the beginning to the end of the course. It is also necessary to remember that the processes of selecting, planning, and carrying out the project establish the major arena of learning; the consequent success or failure of the final product is not the measure of how much students gain.

A major pitfall is for students to become stuck in commiseration about how bad, how pervasive, and how hard racism is to confront rather than focusing on problem solving. Although increased awareness of racism and an ability to identify its manifestations are signs of growth, there is a temptation to engage in condemning racism within the safety of the classroom instead of taking risks by challenging it in the world outside the classroom. Therefore, while acknowledging the students' expanding abilities to identify the myriad expressions of racism correctly, the instructors must focus them on actions aimed at solving problems.

When students first hear about the action-project requirement, they typically feel apprehensive and unskilled. Some consider dropping the course because "I just don't see how I will find time to do anything." Many students will need help getting started. These include the ones who constantly change their minds about projects or suggest unacceptable projects that either do not address the issue of racism or target inappropriate populations. Unless their choices are organic to their present work, they will have difficulty carrying out successful projects. Our goal is to help each identify a small project that relates to some aspect of work or community. If they want to focus on children, we ask them also to include adults such as parents or staff. We also encourage White students to work with Whites rather than to go as missionaries to a community of color.

Action projects vary considerably, depending on students' awareness, confidence, skill, and available time. The context in which they work—including possibilities, limitations, and obstacles—is also significant. Projects have included—

- Involving colleagues in critiquing and changing the collection of children's books in a child development center
- Integrating a culturally relevant approach and/or anti-bias education into an ongoing preschool curriculum
- Providing workshops for parents and colleagues
- Setting up a staff committee to review/change hiring practices
- Becoming involved with a community organization advocating a specific anti-racism issue

Each semester we have a few students who are not quite ready to work directly with other adults. With our permission, these students do a project focused on themselves or their family (e.g., buying diversity-rich materials for their own children or creating a scrapbook of stereotypic and racist images from children's book, magazines, and TV programs). Although we do not encourage this kind of project, we recognize that it is necessary for the occasional student for whom working with others might do more harm than good.

As students formulate plans, their initial apprehension abates. However, new and more serious anxieties arise. Some become aware that integrating anti-racist action into their lives includes risks and may even require fundamental changes in life-style. In wrestling with these anxieties, they confront the basic choice confronting the entire class: whether to remain part of the problem (of which they now have a clearer and deeper picture) or become part of the solution.

Once projects are under way, both instructors and students have more fun, even though other problems arise. Students cast their pebbles into the water, and, armed with newly discovered truths, usually find to their dismay that confronting racism is a lot harder than they had anticipated. To emphasize just how taboo raising questions about racism can be, it is necessary to remember that students' projects are hardly what might be considered militant or radical actions. For example, one student in charge of organizing in-service training for doctors in a large hospital became the target of constant teasing and snide remarks after bringing in a speaker who talked about culturally relevant health care practices. She had previously worked in relative anonymity, and her new visibility made her feel like she was under a microscope, resulting in a sense of tension and harassment. In another case, a student working in a private school for young children made a presentation to staff about racism in children's books. She found that her master teacher responded to the presentation with anger and hostility, and their relationship underwent a dramatic change for the worse. More serious but fortunately not a frequent occurrence, one Black student working in a private social service agency lost her job because of her efforts to implement a more culturally sensitive approach to clients.

Although we are upset that our students face these difficulties, we know that they are an unfortunate but real part of doing anti-racism work. Class discussions help students learn to cope with hostility, criticism, and rejection while encouraging patience and persistence in their work. We draw from our own experiences as anti-racist activists in our work and communities to help students use a range of situation-appropriate strategy and tactics.

ACTIVITIES

The last three sessions of the course expand students' knowledge of the issues, strategies, and problems that are part of anti-racist work, and we also prepare them for the end of the course.

Week 13: Activist Role Models for Anti-Racism

For this session, we invite two or three educators and human service practitioners who are known for their exemplary anti-racism work to talk about their experiences. Because it is important for our students to see anti-racist activists as "real" people committed to the kind of lifelong work we hope the students will also commit to, we emphasize both their personal and their professional sides in this encounter. We select individuals, both people of color and Whites, from southern California communities and ask them to address what they are doing and why, strategies they have found effective and ineffective, challenges/obstacles and how they cope with them, results of their work, and how they keep themselves going.

In our teaching approach, we begin with introductions and then give each resource person 15 to 20 minutes to talk. Usually, we withhold comments and questions until later. After the presentations, we schedule a 15-minute break during which students have an opportunity to talk with the guests individually. When the class reconvenes, the instructors lead a discussion and direct student questions to the guests.

Week 14: Evaluating Action Projects

This session focuses on the action projects students have been doing in their work settings and/or community.

Activity 1: Reports to Support Groups. The peer support groups meet for the last time to hear about the progress and results of each student's action project. Students prepare written summaries before class, describing what has occurred to date and evaluating their work—its strengths and weaknesses, what they have learned, and ideas for follow-through. In turn, each makes a 20-minute presentation to the other members of the support group and elicits questions and suggestions regarding further growth. If they wish, students may incorporate this feedback into their final written report and return the revised draft the following week. Last, they share the changes they perceive in themselves as a result of taking action and make observations about the positive changes that have occurred in each other.

Activity 2: Report to Class of Action Projects' Strategies and Challenges. The whole class reconvenes, and each support group presents a summary of the various issues and strategies of that group's projects. A theme that typically arises during this discussion is the different kinds of resistance students met as they instituted anti-racist approaches in their work, such as trivialization, joking, rudeness, or hostility. Sharing ideas for handling these various types of resistance becomes very empowering as students draw strength from each other's and the instructors' experiences.

In our teaching approach, the role of the instructor is to serve as facilitator, making certain that the discussions stay on track and that everyone has an opportunity to participate. Moreover, we seek to help students understand that, while difficult and not always successful, taking action against racism is not only possible but necessary for gaining a sense of personal liberation from an oppressive system.

Week 15: Where Do We Go from Here?

By now the students have spent extensive and intensive time with each other and feel a strong sense of camaraderie. Students begin to show signs of separation anxiety because the class has become a support group for them, and they recognize how much more they have to learn. Despite students' impressive growth, the topic of racism has not been exhausted, nor is the process of becoming anti-racist completed. They are also concerned about how to find alternative information resources about racism and pro-racism and how to create a support group for themselves outside the class. Thus, students struggle with the class closing as both an ending and a new beginning.

To help us in evaluating their growth, students submit a written self-evaluation describing what they feel they gained from the course and what they feel they contributed to the course. The college does not require us to give letter grades for student evaluations, but it expects narrative comments. We therefore take students' self-reflective thoughts into account as we write end-of-the-semester evaluations.

Activity 1: Reviewing Strategies and Resources. In this last session of the course, we begin by convening the whole class for a review of the paradigm introduced during the fourth week, which defines the different forms of racism. It now serves as a framework for considering strategies in the context of the types of racism and the organizational settings in which people work. We brainstorm about all the various possibilities for appropriate action that students have used or heard about, listing them on a flip-chart or chalk board. Then we relate them to specific contexts. For example, behavioral racism in an organization with non-hierarchical relationships is usually most effectively dealt with through consciousness-raising and peer group action. In contrast, making changes in a hierarchical institution often requires grass-roots education and organizing to influence people of power at the top. We encourage students to consider all kinds of individual and group methods and to choose strategies appropriate to the specific requirements of each concrete issue and contextual factor in which they work. We also highlight alternative sources of information they can continue to use after the course; for example, journals, newspapers, bookstores, organizations, and ways to create or find anti-racist networks, many of which have been discovered by students themselves during the course of the semester.

Activity 2: What Has the Course Meant to You? Students take turns speaking about what the course has meant to them. This is a moving experience because students acknowledge the growth they have seen in themselves and how they have transformed their earlier anxieties, defensiveness, and emotional turmoil into new perspectives and behaviors. As one student described the session, "It is like a purification rite in which we all come back together again and could feel our common humanity and our power. My faith in people being able to change has been renewed."

Our teaching strategy for the second activity is to help students appreciate that they have gained a pivotal life experience as well as completion of a course and, moreover, that they are at the beginning of a lifelong journey. Lecture-style comments by instructors are not necessary. Simply leading the class discussion and encouraging students to comment about what the course has meant provide an eloquent conclusion to the semester.

Individual classmates commit to keeping in touch with each other, and we distribute a telephone list to everyone. Although many students wish otherwise, the class does not provide an ongoing networking arrangement. Periodically, we have discussed the desirability or possibility of building an ongoing "alumni" organization through which graduates of the course could continue to gain support and ideas for carrying out anti-racist work in their communities and job settings. One small group was formed by students who remained at Pacific Oaks College & Children's School as students, parents, or faculty. By the time they completed their second year, they had developed a workshop about helping children develop positive racial identity and anti-racist attitudes, which they presented to many groups of parents and to college-level child development classes. Moreover, this group actively participated in anti-racism work on campus.

STUDENT RESPONSES

In a departure in style from previous chapters where the discussions appear separately, we discuss the responses of students of color and Whites together in this last chapter. This choice serves to show how much in common we all have once committed to activism and to punctuate the fact that, although the two groups of students experience separate journeys, they arrive at the same destination.

Practicing Anti-Racist Behavior

Although more common an experience among students of color than Whites, few students had confronted racism in institutions. Indeed, for those who have never participated in any kind of social action, learning the requisite skills and taking the inherent risks does not happen easily. The issue of power to create change is a predominant struggle for the students:

> I would like to teach myself that I actually have power to effect change on this world for the better. I guess I just have to believe I can do that; that I'm not powerless as I have believed myself most of my life. And the only way I will learn is to try.

Even to take mild action, students must come to grips with their discomfort about confrontation. Repeatedly, they wrote about how expressing criticism and anger was difficult, evoking feelings of great anxiety and discomfort. No matter the level of confrontation—from gently criticizing another person's racist statements to making demands on people in authority—most said that confrontation was considered unpleasant or that they had learned that it was "not nice" or not safe. Many spoke of having been taught to avoid confrontation whenever possible, as if they feared exposing the fragility of people, themselves included, in a way that might result in some sort of interpersonal disaster.

However, they also agreed that, without confrontation of some kind, anti-racism work was impossible. Therefore, coming to grips with fears about confrontation produced growth. Barbara describes the effect of a class session in which a confrontation between a Black and a White and then between two White students took place, followed by a class discussion of these incidents:

> If I had to pick one turning point for myself, it was the discussion we had after the confrontations. I finally faced many of my worst dreads around confrontation, finding I could handle them. In fact, during dinner I felt really comfortable, more so than I ever have felt in this class. But also for the first time, I felt a strong, warm solidarity with all the members of the class. I sensed that we all cared strongly about something together and were working together. Because we cared so much, we were even willing to say the hard stuff to one another.

Another factor contributing to apprehension about taking anti-racist action, especially for White students, involves fear of self-exposure. Discussing her fears about being required to do an action project, Judy explained that

> I had a lot of ambivalence in approaching my project. I finally got in touch with another student with experience in similar work to get help in starting. When Linda said one of her biggest fears was of revealing her own racism, I realized that was true for me too. Once I could talk openly about this, at least one of my fears was alleviated.

Further, our students' anxiety about how other Whites will respond to them if they engage in anti-racist activity is yet another obstacle to overcome. Even before White students have had any experience, they anticipate that White responses will include hostility, rejection, and ostracism. Moreover, once White students begin to confront other Whites, they do in fact discover that there is considerable resistance. Therefore, students need to articulate their anxieties about these responses and struggle to find strategies for handling defensiveness, anger, and other forms of resistance. Since we believe Whites' primary job is to change the racist attitudes and behaviors manifested by other Whites, they must learn to cope with feelings engendered by negative responses from family, friends, and colleagues. The journals of White students present many illustrations of this issue. Martha writes:

I am trying to talk with my family and friends about racism without losing them or getting disinherited. So far, it hasn't been working very well. There are some people you can approach on touchy subjects and plant a seed for thought, and then there are those who reject it without the least bit of thought. I can see it's going to be a very strategic game.

Frank finds that

teaching my racism class to high schoolers is a real experience. I am constantly being faced with comments like "Our kids aren't prejudiced at all so I don't know why you teach a whole course about it" or "You're teaching a course about racism, so suddenly you're imagining it everywhere now."

Ann reveals the feelings she felt in response to the resistance she met from fellow church members:

I introduced the idea of showing one of the films we saw in class to a group of Christian service people with whom I work. The response was startling to me. They became quiet as I described the history of making the film and how it was confiscated by the government. When I discussed the topic of the film, they became so uncomfortable and threatened that I almost got thrown out of the meeting. Most of them tried to convince me that racism is hardly an issue in this country. Although I know lack of awareness of racism is a major factor in its perpetuation, it still surprises me, baffles me, and angers me when I discover the ignorance and complacency of well-meaning people.

Students of color must jump similar hurdles to avoid being immobilized by negative responses to their attempts at anti-racist practice. Furthermore, reality-based fear of retribution compounds their anxiety because society has dealt harshly with activists of color who have challenged White control and power. Journal entries echo disturbing memories of stories about what happens to those who openly take a stand:

I know I had learned by the age of six not to say anything about what I thought concerning racial injustice. I think part of my silence came from my feeling really scared once when my family went to a civil rights rally. When we got back to the car, all the windows were broken out. I remember being scared because until then I had only seen violence on television, and I thought things like that could only happen in the South.

These issues are essential topics for class discussion, because we want students to practice anti-racist activity in spite of the possible problems and dangers. Students sometimes exaggerate their apprehensions, but they are not unrealistic or unreasonable. It would be a disservice to them to pretend that there will never be any negative repercussions. Nevertheless, it would also be a disservice to the children and adults with whom they work as human service professionals if they failed to embrace an anti-racist perspective. Thus, even though previous contradictions and tensions have been resolved, becoming anti-racist raises new challenges that will require a lifelong commitment.

Being an Anti-Racist Activist

After beginning to discuss racism with family, friends, and colleagues, students find themselves accused of being too radical or too militant. They then must consider their own definitions of these terms. "I used to think of militant activists as obnoxious," declared Ruth:

> They might be fighting for a worthy cause; yet they always seemed somehow arrogant to me, and I would avoid them for fear of being cussed out or treated like dirt. I never would have believed I'd be where I am now. Now other people are scared of me, thinking I'm threatening, crazy, or overly concerned about nothing. They think I'm going through a phase and will grow out of it. But I won't. I feel a strong sense of solidarity with all people of color, and know that we're all in this together, both the unaware and the aware.

Realizing that eliminating racism requires a long-term commitment, students think about how they will sustain their commitment to anti-racism in the future. Barbara, who jokingly remarked "Too bad we can't take energy capsules to get us all through," also maintained in her final journal entry that

> I've been giving much thought to Ana's [a Chicana] remarks a few weeks ago that Whites can leave the class and choose whether or not to do anti-racist work. But I feel it is no longer a choice for me. I feel my integrity is on the line. I can be anti-racist or lead a living death, a life without meaning, and I can't think of anything worse.

Unless people can continue to see how working to end racism is in their own interest and not simply a matter of doing a good deed for others, it is unlikely that anti-racism work will either continue or be effective. A critical issue is whether students will be able to find or create support networks for themselves. Martha expresses this concern when she states:

Next week is our last class, and though I usually feel relieved and like celebrating at the end of a semester, this class is different. I'm going to miss the people, and I don't really want to say a good-bye. I realize that I'm going to have to find support elsewhere and know that it's going to be a difficult task for me. I am feeling lost about where I belong as a White anti-racist. Where is my community? Not with the racists and not with the oppressed. Where?

As students perceive that they themselves have changed as they take beginning steps toward activism, they feel a growing sense of enjoyment:

When I began this course, I felt doomed. Doomed forever to being racist and saying racist things. I thought change was impossible in me or anyone. I have found that I could really learn enough to change and to help others to do some changing, and it wasn't all hard. Learning to be anti-racist could also be fun.

Ana explains how her action project was decisive for her:

Involvement in my action project has changed me from a passive person to an activist. It took a great deal of courage for me to get involved both physically and emotionally, and I realize that one doesn't have to be able to change the whole world oneself. As an activist, I belong to a Latina woman's group, am a contributing member of ACLU, send telegrams to the President, join boycotts, and lead a support group for undocumented immigrants. Being an activist is a much better place to be.

A dialectic emerges between anti-racist activity and enhanced self-concept:

The most astonishing of the changes I have made is that I have begun to confront others on racist issues. I'm no longer afraid to discuss my point of view with others or to have a point of view. At least I'm beginning to sound like I really know what I'm talking about and to do something about it. This class has definitely built up my self-esteem.

Students discover the satisfaction of making a clear statement about what you believe, having new knowledge and words to express yourself, and above all taking a stand:

I feel that I'm taking an active part in what happens in my city, state, and country. This is the kind of contribution I want to make to change the future for children of color and all children. I'm getting less and less afraid to speak out for what I believe in and what I think. I've learned a lot about myself and about standing up for myself and for others.

Through practicing anti-racism, sharing ideas, and evaluating their experiences with classmates, students begin to discover how to work effectively with others. One student offered what is perhaps the best summary about doing anti-racist work:

> I'm finally finding ways to communicate in a way that keeps people's walls down and not up. You can't be a broken record; you'll lose them. You can't cut their throats to force them to listen. It has to be a belief, a language, and behaviors that work in different settings and for different levels of awareness. This skill is the hardest. You can't read it in the book. It is a skill that comes with time commitment and intuition for each separate situation.

Experiencing Anti-Racism as Personal Liberation

Perhaps the most moving of the changes that appear as the semester ends is one that we had neither anticipated nor included in the list of objectives—a rejuvenated, renewed sense of personal freedom:

> I am happier now than I have ever been—I am a liberated Chicana now. I know who I am, who my enemy is, what the enemy is doing to my people, when to fight, when to stop fighting, and what form the struggle must take.

All aspects of students' lives are touched. "This class has begun to accomplish so much in the freeing of my soul," one student reports. This theme is echoed by many in their final journal pages:

> I think this class has in some way, large or small, touched every facet of my life. It has challenged or strengthened most of my values, giving me new standards by which to judge all that I read or see, hear or say. It has given me new horizons toward which to grow. I listen with better educated ears, read more critically, debate with more ease. I came into this class expecting that an acknowledgment of my ignorance, along with an apology for it, would get me off the hook. Well, I am no longer ignorant and therefore unable to use that excuse. From here on in, the responsibility rests with me to be informed and in some way active.

Why does anti-racism education arouse such feelings for both students of color and for Whites? Perhaps the answer lies in Memmi's (1965) observation that "for me oppression is the greatest calamity of humanity: it diverts and pollutes the best energies of men [and women], of oppressor and oppressed alike" (p. xvii). Becoming anti-racist empowers people to restore and redirect the energy for humane instead of inhumane ends, for growth rather than atrophy.

Students write about the personal freeing they experience in many ways:

> Tonight was our last class. I've been thinking about why it affects people so much. I think it's because, in untying the knot, you're unraveling the web of lies that each of us has inevitably experienced, and racism is only a part of the false information each of us received while growing up. Racism is the part that is most obvious and blatant. There are many other parts that have taken their dehumanizing toll, and, in unraveling even a bit of the whole, we feel tremendously excited. We have only to unravel more of it to reclaim ourselves more completely.

It is not surprising that students of color find shedding pro-racist beliefs and behaviors to be personally freeing. After all, each trait of pro-racist consciousness results in alienation from an essential part of oneself and reinforcement of one's own oppression. It is more surprising, at least at first glance, that White students also write compellingly about their increased self-esteem and sense of personal freedom. After all, racism favors them. But what they discover is the immensely more powerful freeing effects that anti-racism education offers to heal their mind-heart-conscience split and to end the toxic psychological effects of the creed-deed discrepancy. So for Whites becoming anti-racist is also a reintegration process. "Now there is a feeling inside me which I can only describe as a heavy weight being lifted." The considerable energy students have used to contain or repress the tensions racism creates is now available for acting on one's convictions. Along with the opportunity to become more psychologically whole, anti-racism education enables students to gain a more realistic sense of self by demystifying the interaction between the individual and the social system. One student's moving statement captures how many feel: "I feel as if a veil has been torn from my eyes and that I understand myself and my world for the first time. This is the kind of education I have been seeking for years."

Having more powerful tools for understanding their society is particularly pertinent to human service practitioners since their work is frequently filled with frustrations at not being successful in helping an individual child or adult as much as they want. It is useful to be able to identify sources beyond one's own inadequacies or the weaknesses of the people with whom one works. Self-blame leads to feelings of low self-esteem and burnout; faulting the clients leads to victim-blaming, cynicism, and poor services. Having the analytic tools for identifying institutional constraints also opens the door to institutional solutions. Thus, we are back to our opening parable in the Introduction: Anti-racism education frees people to be actors—to challenge rather than to acquiesce in social oppression.

CONCLUSION

Before we leave the course, we raise one last question: How much will any of this matter? Is there any lasting consequence of these experiences? Do students, after 2 or 5 or even 10 years, remain activists?

We have no formal study to give us the answer. Yet, in Pasadena where all of this started, many of us involved in anti-racism education still live and work, and can make observations about the activities of former students. In addition, though scattered across the country, others are engaged in early childhood and human service work. In both these circles, news about former students travels quickly.

We knew about those who have kept in touch for support and advice as they carried out projects that would become central to their professional careers. Among them have emerged leaders in the "anti-bias movement." Several have written children's books to counteract the racial, gender, and other stereotypes in the literature and to fill voids in subject, story theme, and character portrayals. Some have written books for adults about strategies for achieving anti-racist consciousness and practice. Many have begun and continue to lead projects at their work sites to change personnel policies, organize and lead homogeneous support groups, and establish study groups. Yet others have become entrepreneurs—consulting, conducting workshops, and producing products for use in early care and education settings.

Perhaps less visible but of no less significance are those who live in a new and transformed way, raising their children and interacting with their colleagues differently, they believe, as a result of the class. We know about them and their thoughts on the consequences of the class over time because we wrote to former students and asked them. In response they reported that the imprint of the class had been long-lasting.

In particular, the things they remembered most about the class were the support they felt, the straightforward approach to the topic, the honesty and openness of classmates, and their powerful and conflicting emotions. They said:

Never before or since have I been asked to confront such taboo issues.

Thanks to the fear from which that class freed me, I have been able ever since to speak up and speak out.

I still draw strength today from the courage of my fellow students in that class.

I'll never forget the gut-wrenching pain I went through, nor how much support I got from the instructors to get through it all.

Finally, the profound mark that the class experience leaves on people's lives is expressed over and over in the letters we receive. Some describe how former students have used the class books and reading materials repeatedly in their work. Others describe how they have used repeatedly the principles they learned. Mostly, however, people told us that their lives had been changed:

> The training in the class was the cornerstone in my commitment to social justice. This commitment is now integrated into my total life and way of viewing the world, not just my professional life. It changed the way I raise my children and relate to my family. I will remain ever grateful that I can now think of myself as a self-respecting person.

PART III

How to Adapt the Course

People who believe, as do we, that learning how to become anti-racist is possible for individuals realize that courses in anti-racism are needed throughout our society. Besides conducting the course described in this book—where students are preparing for careers in teaching, early childhood development, and other human services professions—the authors have collaborated with and served as consultants to other groups through the United States where the participants or learning context is different from what we describe in the book.

In our interaction with representatives of other communities and educational institutions, we have observed that the phases of student self-discovery and transformation are valid in other settings. However, some of the teaching methods, materials, and class schedules may need to be adapted. In Chapter 7, we address how to pursue the teaching role and adapt the course to your own needs.

CHAPTER 7

Making the Course Your Own

In this chapter we discuss issues related to teaching your own anti-racism course. First we reflect on the following dimensions of the teaching role: (1) interracial team teaching, (2) stresses and ways of coping, (3) teacher as learner, (4) continuing self-education. Second we consider factors to take into account when adapting or contextualizing our approach to various settings.

REFLECTIONS ON TEACHING

Each semester, at least one student asks Carol how, as a Black person, she can stand to teach the racism course semester after semester and be regularly subjected to students' racist remarks. Her response to one of these queries succinctly delineates the role of the teacher in anti-racism education:

> I believe that everyone *can* learn to be anti-racist. That's why I teach this class. Whether people want to or not is part of the challenge of teaching this class well, to help people want to change. My role, thus, is as both empathizer and antagonist. At times I must be teacher/facilitator, at other times critic. My task is to time these in such a way as to help you grow and change and to interpret your reactions to me so as to help me grow and change in the way I teach.

There are no recipes. The delicate interplay between the two roles of antagonist and empathizer unfolds throughout the progression of students' growth. Depending on either an individual or the group's developmental needs, one role or the other will be at the fore in response to what is occurring.

Interracial Team Teaching

Our model of teaching and learning requires an interracial teaching team. The dual perspectives gained from living as a member of the dominant or dominated within our society results in a deeper understanding of racism, richer and more relevant interactions with students, a more accurate assessment of students' needs and progress, and more empathetic awareness of the process students experience as they become anti-racist.

Working to achieve agreement between ourselves about appropriate expectations, techniques, and content has been the arena within which our understanding of anti-racism education evolved. For example, learning to productively handle the guilt-anger syndrome of the conflict period resulted from numerous conversations about our initially different responses to this issue. It was easier for Louise to sympathize with the White students' pain and to help them work out their guilt feelings than it was for Carol, who tended to minimize such feelings and be impatient with them. Conversely, Carol was able to identify the trap in students of color's ventilation of anger without also taking responsibility for acting against racism, while Louise got caught in encouraging expressions of anger without pushing further. Each of us had to learn from the perspectives and skills of the other in order to be able to effectively help students work through the difficult conflict period.

We do not always have the same analysis about every aspect of racism, either, and express differing views as they come up. This heightens students' awareness of the complexity involved in analyzing all of racism's manifold manifestations and models the kind of interaction in which we want them to engage. An interracial team also enables students to identify with anti-racist role models from their own and other groups, enabling them to gain deeper understanding of the role members of each group play. Moreover, for most of our students, this is the first time they have gotten to know a white anti-racist or, particularly for students of color, have had the opportunity to work on issues of racism with a teacher of color.

All team-teaching situations require careful attention to how power is shared. Ongoing communication, negotiation, and evaluation are essential. Interracial team teaching carries an added responsibility—paying attention to the social as well as the personal meanings of behavior. Chester Pierce (1980) reminds us of the importance of the daily seemingly insignificant interactions between whites and people of color that undergird unequal racial relationships. Therefore, it is not only necessary to monitor how the more obvious teaching tasks are shared (e.g., who gives directions or leads discussions), but it is also necessary to monitor the micro-interactions of which we are not normally aware: Who starts the class, who decides on break time, who brings the group back together, who sets up the physical environment, who makes the coffee (which we provide), who does the most talking, who has the last word, whose group goes to another room when we break up (students are quite conscious of whether the Whites or students of color leave the room when we meet in homogeneous groups, and we insist on taking turns regardless of the size of each group). Moreover, specific class sessions are more appropriately run by one or the other because of the structural or social significance of a particular topic. For example, the institutional racism lecture is always given by Louise since it is Whites who hold institutional power, thereby modeling Whites' taking responsibility for explaining and analyzing racism.

During class discussions, a delicate balance exists between supporting each other, voicing different views, and undercutting one another. On the one hand, one of the advantages of team teaching is being able to come to each other's aid, and given the challenge of always having to be thinking on your feet during interactions with students, aid is occasionally most welcome. We have learned to interpret each other's signals for when one wants the other to take over a particular interaction or group discussion. On the other hand, because our judgments about how to push a particular student differ, we have found it best to not interfere during the interaction, leaving a discussion about what happened until after class when it is possible to find out what each of our perspectives is on that particular student. The following week always provides another chance to work with the student if necessary. Another interaction to watch for is the White teacher's always having the last word.

Unconscious racist interactions will inevitably occur since even instructors of anti-racism education courses do not escape the conditioning of a racist society. Accordingly, regular, critical, and honest discussion of the team's interactions is required regardless of how small a particular issue seems or the potential discomfort caused by these discussions. It is also important to remember that it is the consequence of our behavior, not the intent, that must be examined. Moreover, the different teaching strengths, skills, and styles that each teacher brings to the group must be honored but not used as an excuse for an imbalance of power.

We have been asked if the class can be done by one instructor, rather than an interracial team. Although it is certainly possible, it is not desirable, and would change a key element of our approach. If an interracial team is not available within the faculty, perhaps it is possible to work with someone from outside your setting as a visiting faculty member. Perhaps you can form a diverse teaching team around another aspect of identity (e.g., class, or gender, or sexual orientation, or disability). Even if both teachers are from the same racial or ethnic group, at least such a team brings the strength of different perspectives to help model as well as process the dynamics of the class. Moreover, beyond the rationale we have already described for an interracial teaching team, other, more personal considerations exist. Anti-racism education, as we have repeatedly described it through the preceding chapters, is emotionally challenging for the teacher as well as the student. Working alone does not provide the kind of feedback and support we need to keep us working on our own issues as we guide our students to work on theirs.

Stresses and Ways of Coping

Teaching about racism makes enormous demands on the instructor's personal as well as professional resources. We are dealing with highly charged material that personally affects us, our families, our children, and our friends and that invokes intense emotional responses in us as well as in our students. Developing emotional detachment on the subject is not only impossible, it is inappropriate. However, we do have to develop the self-discipline that enables us to make choices about when and how we express our feelings. Maintaining such self-discipline is one of the most difficult tasks because there is a built-in contradiction in anti-racism teaching. We work hard at creating an atmosphere in which students feel safe to talk openly, yet what students say provokes pain and anger in us. If we permit ourselves to get angry too early, we can create a situation in which students' feelings and ideas go underground again. On the other hand, if we never show anger, we take away a chance for them to learn to cope with the anger that their racist attitudes and behavior provoke. Timing, as we have said earlier, is critical, and it is in the timing that self-discipline becomes so important.

In the beginning of our teaching, we found ourselves getting caught in certain unproductive interactions because of our emotional involvement. These included—

1. Becoming so self-righteous in our perspective that we slipped unawares from facilitating a student's thinking into lecturing with a barrage of words
2. Writing off individual students too soon, rather than searching for ways to get past their resistance and defensiveness
3. Closing some students up by expressing anger too early

These three types of unproductive responses typically occur when we leap too quickly into an "I'm going to tell you" mode rather than taking the time to find out more of how a student is thinking, and to then see if, through further questioning, the student can begin to understand the hurtful and/or misinformed implications of what he or she is saying. Knowing what "pushes our buttons" most as a result of experience helps in gaining and maintaining self-discipline. Most important, however, was our increasing understanding of the students' phases of growth, which gave us cognitive tools for judging when to be empathetic and when to be antagonist, when to hide our feelings and when to reveal them. Learning from experience that students could and did indeed change made us feel that the hard work involved in disciplining ourselves paid off.

Risk taking is also as inevitable for teachers as it is for students. Because there are no easy recipes, from time to time it is impossible to avoid experiencing anxiety or unsureness about how to proceed in a given interaction with a student or the whole class. In fact, in the beginning of our teaching, it sometimes felt more like being out of control than just unsureness. Over the years, as we have gained more clarity about what is happening for students, we became more comfortable about flowing with whatever arises. However, even after many years of teaching, incidents occur that present new challenges or that we wish we had handled differently. As we have become more confident about our work, and more cognizant of how deeply racism affects everyone, we have been less embarrassed by our mistakes. Making mistakes never feels good, but we no longer lose a night's sleep, as we did at first.

Because the outcome of this course matters so deeply, coping with the reality that we are not able to stimulate and inspire growth in all students is yet another source of stress. We are never really reconciled to this frustration and keep searching for further techniques and understanding of the factors that produce anti-racist consciousness and behavior. However, we have learned to accept the reality of students' leaving the class at different places in their journey, and to accept losing a few students each semester with more grace. We have also learned that in some cases the fruits of taking the course do not appear immediately.

There is no doubt that teaching anti-racism classes is draining. It is important to have people, in addition to each other, who can provide ongoing support, people with whom we can discuss and evaluate specific classroom interactions and brainstorm teaching methods and who can remind us of the significance of our work. Spouses, partners, and children can get some of the emotional fallout. It helps if they understand some of the stresses we experience. Finally, working with other people doing anti-racist work enables us to continue our own development as anti-racists and to make ongoing links between our educational work in the classroom and the larger struggle to eliminate racism.

Despite the stresses however, we want to clearly state that we find anti-racism teaching exhilarating. When we see growth in students, especially when they achieve the transformational phase, the hard work is more than made up for.

Teacher as Learner

We believe that there are three essential prerequisites for teaching an anti-racism course: (1) a belief that racism sabotages effective human service work; (2) a desire to challenge racism; and (3) a willingness to take risks, be self-introspective, and learn from mistakes. This book provides teachers with the next three essential ingredients: (1) background information about the dynamics of racism (with further suggested readings); (2) the developmental framework of students' patterns and progressions of growth; and (3) specific ideas and techniques for activities. Skills are refined and deepened by taking the plunge first, and then building on that beginning. So, throughout one's involvement with anti-racism education, one must continue to be a learner. Our understanding of racism and of ourselves and our teaching skills are enriched and improved with each succeeding teaching experience. Over the years we have also become more familiar with the work of other anti-racism educators. Reading accounts of their experiences when available and engaging in personal communication when possible have become valuable avenues for improving our own work. Moreover, social forces in our society and in the world at large change the specific dynamic of racism and highly different issues around which struggle revolves. It is vital to keep abreast of what is happening and to modify course content as necessary.

The teacher-as-learner concept also embodies a key assumption of our pedagogical model: that there are no bystanders in the education process. Although as teachers we provide leadership in the course, we are still faced with the same contradictions racism creates for our students. Their struggle to become and live as anti-racists is the teachers' struggle as well. Although the teachers may have invested more time in becoming aware of and knowledgeable about issues that many of the students have not yet even realized are significant, once the process of development begins, students have a great deal to learn from each other and to teach the teachers. The instructors must provide leadership, but not act as if they have completed, once and for all, their journey as anti-racists. Rather, it is vital that the teachers share with students their own personal struggles in dealing with racism, their mistakes as well as their successes. So doing frees students to take risks and makes the task of becoming anti-racist seem less insurmountable.

CONTINUING SELF-EDUCATION

We have found it vital to continue our own self-education. The following activities for us are musts.

Enrolling in Workshops of Other Anti-Racism Training Groups

This provides opportunities to grow by working on one's own identity and racism issues. Further, one learns both from other trainers' content and from their instructional strategies. It is also helpful to experience being in the student role.

While these opportunities exist all across the country (and in the international community as well), some we have found exemplary are listed below. Each group has somewhat different focus and methods, but all are within the general ball park of anti-racism education.

People's Institute for Survival and Beyond
144 North Johnson Street
New Orleans, LA 70116-1767
phone (504) 944-2354

Crossroads Ministry
425 S. Central Park Avenue
Chicago, IL 60624
phone (312) 638-0166

Communitas, Inc.
245 Main Street
Northhampton, MA 01060
phone (413) 586-3088

National Multicultural Institute
3000 Connecticut Ave N.W., Suite 438
Washington, DC 20008-2556
phone (202) 483-0700

Visions, Inc.
545 Concord Avenue, Suite 1
Cambridge, MA 02138
phone (617) 876-9257

Forming a Support Group with Other Educators Teaching Anti-Racism Classes

This can serve as a way to exchange information and teaching techniques, work on personal issues that arise during your teaching, and help to keep motivation high.

Support groups can come together in various ways: Ask colleagues in your own department, in your community, or in your local professional organization. Six to eight people is a desirable size, but remember that even two people can constitute themselves as an ongoing "buddy" relationship. A support group is made up of peers who relate their experiences, do reflection together, provide feedback and support, help each other solve problems, study together. Mutual respect and caring that grow out of this kind of support go a long way toward supplying the inspiration and energy that anti-racism leadership requires.

Keeping Up with Current Literature

Keeping aware of new books on racism requires initiative because many commercial bookstores either do not stock or have only a limited selection of these works. Locate and periodically browse in bookstores in your city that carry a wide and updated selection of books about racism. These may be found in smaller community-based bookstores that specialize in specific ethnic groups of color and in more "alternative" or "radical" bookstores located outside of main commercial areas (e.g., malls).

Subscribing to periodicals that address issues of equity and diversity is another way to keep informed about new materials. We have found the following newsletters particularly helpful:

Teaching Tolerance
400 Washington Avenue
Montgomery, AL 36104
fax (334) 264-3121

Rethinking Schools
1001 East Keefe Avenue
Milwaukee, WI 53212
phone (414) 964-9646

Multicultural Education
Caddo Gap Press
3145 Geary Boulevard, #275
San Francisco, CA 94118
phone (415) 750-9978

Joining Organizations

Several national organizations focus on equity, cultural and multicultural issues
in education. Joining them provides access to yearly conferences (which, in addition to offering workshops, have publisher displays of current books), newsletters
or journals, and networking. Such organizations include the following:

National Association of Bilingual Education
1220 L. Street, N.W., Suite 605
Washington, DC 20005-4018
phone (202) 898-1829

Teaching Tolerance
400 Washington Avenue
Montgomery AL 36104
fax (334) 264-3121

National Association of Multicultural Education
1511 K. Street, N.W., Suite 430
Washington, DC 20005
phone (202) 628-6263

National Black Child Development Institute
1023 15th Street, N.W., Suite 600
Washington, DC 20005
phone (202) 387-1281

National Coalition of Educational Activists
Box 679
Rhinebrook, NY 12572-0679

Surfing the Internet

Many resources are becoming available on the Internet. There are dozens of World Wide Web sites dedicated in whole or in part to anti-racism information, multiculturalism, and related social justice issues. There are additional sites focusing on the interests of specific peoples of color—African American, Asian American, Native American, Mexican American, other dominated groups in the United States, and people in the Third World who are dominated by a Euro-American culture and economy. Most of the culture-specific web sites are developed and maintained by individuals who belong to the featured cultural group, and some of the sites provide an excellent means for learning about cultures, history, current issues, and contributions by contemporary thinkers, artists, and activists. As with the Internet generally, the quality of specific sites will vary from excellent to poor, and you will have to exercise your own judgment about which sites to use.

We have not provided "addresses" for specific web sites because they often change, and new sites become available frequently. Instead, we suggest you use the web search engines such as Yahoo, Webcrawler, Alta Vista, HotBot, and Lycos. In searching, we have found that productive key words include *anti-racism*, *racism*, *sexism*, *multicultural*, as well as the names of specific groups (e.g., *Native American*).

The Internet also has "news groups" that function as electronic bulletin boards, providing news, opinions, articles, and both facts and lies. Deja News and Alta Vista have excellent keyword search capabilities. Besides looking for positive information about anti-racism, you can locate examples of hate, racism, anti-Semitism, and sexism discussed openly (often rudely and profanely) by using such search phrases as *white supremacy*, *white power*, *white men*, *sexism against men*, *holocaust myth*, and racial epithets. As Internet access becomes common, your students will also be able to locate examples of quality anti-racism resources and the seamy messages of prejudiced minds.

PARTICIPATING IN ANTI-RACIST ACTIVITY

Teaching from a position of asking students to "do what I say, not what I do," doesn't work in our approach to anti-racism education. Instead the teacher role-models personal change and commitment. Participating in social change, moreover, has an effect on the teacher similar to that on the students, vitalizing one's understanding of racism and of what it means to resist rather than acquiesce. Such learning does not come from books.

Continual growth is essential to an anti-racism educator. Each group of learners raises variations on general themes that challenge us to hone our skills at the same time new insights about ourselves suggest additional paths for self-development.

ADAPTING THE COURSE TO DIFFERENT SETTINGS

Our approach to anti-racism education was shaped in interaction with the population of educators and human service practitioners for whom our course was designed. Thus, adapting the course requires a cognizance of particular learner groups. Key factors to weigh when considering activities and content include (1) characteristics of students, (2) setting, and (3) current faces of racism.

Characteristics of Students

Several dimensions of the makeup of the student population influence our decisions about pedagogy, including their racial/ethnic composition, ideology, and work and educational background. We discuss these below.

Racial/Ethnic Composition of the Group. The racial/ethnic composition of the group with which one works carries both political and pedagogical implications. Some anti-racism educators make a cogent case for racially homogeneous groups as the appropriate format. The main advantage is that Whites, on the one hand, and people of color, on the other, can work on their own issues free of the problems and distractions that occur in interracial groups. Separate groups give people of color the opportunity to immerse themselves in reclaiming their own identity and heritage and reinforce for Whites the importance of acknowledging that racism is an essentially White problem and of finding ways to support each other in the task of becoming accountable for its elimination. A modification of the homogeneous group that some also use is to have each group first meet separately and then, after a number of separate sessions, meet together to explore ways of forming alliances.

We have opted to use an integrated group format because we believe that a coalition of anti-racist Whites and people of color is necessary for ending racism and that pedagogically an interracial group more closely resembles the work situations most of our students will enter or are already in and therefore more effectively provides the dynamics that students must learn to face and work through. However, we do agree that there are some very difficult issues and group dynamics that must be carefully monitored and guided in interracial groups. Particular care must be given to meeting the needs of both groups. There must be clarity about the different tasks for Whites and students of color in their journey toward anti-racism and structures that enable both groups to master them. White students must not be allowed to focus their learning on other groups. They are in the course to help themselves, not to help the poor victims of racism. Conversely, students of color, while needing to spend considerable time learning about their own group, also need to address themselves to learning about the cultures of other groups oppressed by racism and understanding how racism also affects Whites.

The racial composition of the groups we have worked with has varied each semester, ranging anywhere from a 60 to 40 ratio of Whites to people of color to a 90 to 10 ratio. One semester, only White students registered, so we wound up working with an all-White group. We have found that the course works most easily, though not necessarily most successfully in terms of overall students' growth, with a 60 to 40 or 70 to 30 ratio. In this situation, the reality of different perspectives coming from different structural positions of racism is more readily apparent. Students of color feel safer about openly sharing their experiences and viewpoints and feelings, knowing they will have backup and support from others who share similar positions. White students have an opportunity, not usual for most, to experience a group dynamic closer to the reality of the world, where Whites are not the numerical majority. They are forced to take other viewpoints more seriously, which facilitates the breakdown of their ethnocentric blinders and enables them to more profoundly understand that Whites too have a specific racial-cultural identity and perspective based on their social context.

In our experience, the group that is most difficult to facilitate is one in which most of the participants are White. In this situation, there is typically great pressure on the sole or few students of color to teach the White students about what it means to be a person of color or to be spokespersons for their group. For students of color, the group is essentially White and they feel much more vulnerable about sharing their feelings and experiences. Teachers have to take extra care to ensure that students of color set their own goals for the course and achieve what is important to them. However, one positive feature of this particular group composition is that divisions between White students can become more obvious as some White students move more quickly than others to an anti-racist perspective.

Can our model be used effectively with either a White-only group or a homogenous group of color? We used it with a small all-White group only once, with one of us teaching the class, and found some important differences in the dynamics of the course. Without direct experience of different life perspectives, resistance to accepting the realities of racism went on longer, and hence the disequilibrium of the second phase occurred considerably later than in the other groups with which we have worked. Consequently, at the end of the semester many students were still in the conflict period, or just making the transition to the next phase of growth. It was also more difficult for the one White instructor to maintain a balance between pushing and supporting, with the confronting role receiving more emphasis as the semester went on. Consulting with another colleague of color was helpful, but bringing her in to do a few classes had its traps. Students tended to put her in the "spokesperson" role, and she did not have the ongoing relationships with students so vital to this work.

Further teaching with other White-only groups would enable us to know if this one experience was characteristic of a particular group of students or of White-only groups in general. We cannot comment on the effectiveness of our model with a homogeneous group of people of color since we have never used it with such a group. Our belief that no model can serve all groups without modification leads us to conclude that modifications would have to be made for the course to be effective with any type of racially/ethnically homogeneous group.

Ideology of the Students. In addition to racial/ethnic composition, the general ideology of the group presents another salient group characteristic. As we described earlier, our students, for the most part, enter the class disliking racism in a general way, even though they themselves are participating in it, often unaware. About one-third take the class voluntarily each semester; the rest are advised to take it to meet competency requirements for a degree. Thus, the majority do not think they need to learn about racism either because they believe it does not concern them or because they believe they are already nonracist. We believe that the Whites we work with are typical of a substantial part of the White population and probably a majority of those who choose human service work—that is, those who dissociate themselves from the more blatant forms of bigotry, believe in a sometimes undefined way that people are people, but in reality have accepted the more subtle aspects of racist ideology and, albeit sometimes unwittingly, participate in maintaining racism. The question we would have to ask is whether our approach would work with Whites who are openly bigoted. Since we do not have experience with this group, we can only speculate as to whether the general framework of our model would be useful. Is it possible to create classroom conditions under which people who espouse bigoted beliefs can identify and acknowledge contradictions in their ideas and behavior, so that their world view is disrupted and they can become open to alternative ways of thinking? Will common class or gender interests provide a baseline or readiness for realizing the contradictions racism poses to the self-interest of both Whites and people of color?

Students' Work and Educational Backgrounds. We can also wonder what modifications would be appropriate if the students of color vary significantly from those with whom we have experience. On the one hand, the pro-racist consciousness of most of our students is characteristic to some extent of a significant portion of the population of color in our society. On the other hand, the progression of development that we have found and that other Black researchers have identified has been based mainly on middle-class adults, who are not representative of the class makeup of a substantial part of the Black community. Thus, again, we can only wonder whether the pedagogy we have evolved would be appropriate outside of college and middle-class or professional settings.

Further, work settings might dictate modification. Although probably the first six weeks of the course should be kept intact, because this part lays the psychological groundwork for new knowledge and behavior, during the second half of the course it is appropriate to modify curriculum content depending on the particular human service areas for which students are preparing. For example, when many of the students plan to teach children, issues such as IQ testing and intelligence, learning styles and language, children's development of racial and cultural identity, and racial prejudice are frequent topics. However, when numbers of students work with adults as therapists, administrators of mental health centers, and parent educators, the discussion includes topics such as the implications of culture for childrearing, family organization, communication, and treatment. A course adapted for social work students would spend more time on the impact of culture and racism on social service systems and delivery. A course directed at health care workers would focus on the specifics of racism in health care settings and cultural implications for prevention and treatment.

In addition, students' levels of education and life experiences will affect choices of specific content, readings, and activities. For example, if students' reading levels pose an obstacle to using the books we suggest, alternative ways to get this content become necessary. Students may work in reading groups, taking only one chapter per group; the teacher may choose to read certain key points and questions to guide sutents' reading. If the student group is young, and has not yet had work experience, it may be useful to bring more practitioners into various parts of the course from week 7 on.

Structural Variables of the Setting

Adapting our course to settings outside of a college, such as in-service courses in schools or human service agencies or for interested individuals in a community or an organization, requires solving a few potential organizational challenges. We consider essential several components that may become problematic in such settings: a commitment of time, regular attendance, staying with the group during rough times, and carrying out an action project.

Because most in-service presentations on race relations typically consist of a 2–3 hour one-time workshop or, sometimes, a 1-day experience, they do not incorporate these elements. In such a short period, it is possible to introduce some new concepts, but not to produce any profound changes in people's consciousness or behavior. It is impossible to implement the dialectic pedagogy at the core of our model in a short time frame. Such attempts can even become counterproductive. If one is successful in provoking disequilibrium, there is usually no time for the next essential task, facilitating the conflict process through to transformation. Instead, the participants are left exposed with intense feelings for which they get no support or help. We have seen the scars left in some individuals who have participated in one-shot, short-time sessions like this. They may even be more defensive about looking at racism than people who have never experienced poorly executed race relations programs. Others simply revert back to their original thinking and little or no impact occurs. Considering that children begin to be socialized into racism by the time they are 3 and 4 years of age, by the time we are adults there is a lot of unlearning to do. Willingness to commit a sufficient length of time to anti-racism education is therefore a key indicator of the seriousness of intent. One-shot workshops are simply token overtures without substance.

Our model demands a considerable period of time. We have used the format of a 3- or 4-hour session per week for 15 weeks. Because developing anti-racism consciousness is transformational rather than linear, it is necessary to have time to experience and productively resolve the issues of each stage of development.

Several exciting examples of long-term anti-racism education efforts illustrate that it can be done when there is serious intent. These range from voluntary community groups who come together for both their own development and to do community advocacy and action, to agency-supported in-service arrangements, to professional organization–supported projects, to church-supported programs. (Examples include the California Association for the Education of Young Children's Leadership-in-Diversity Projects, the Culturally Relevant/Anti-Bias Education Leadership Development Project, the Crossroads Ministry anti-racism project.) Although not all of these efforts use the education model we describe, they all exemplify that it is possible to implement sustained anti-racism education initiatives outside a formal college setting.

Current Sociopolitical Dynamics

Changing sociopolitical dynamics demand new topics and readings. In the session on sexism, classism, and racism (Chapter 5, week 7) we would now also include heterosexism and homophobia, as interconnecting forms of oppression, in terms of their own dynamics and as key elements of sexism. During a period when children from Spanish-speaking ethnic groups are one of the fastest growing populations, we would highlight bilingual education in discussions about culture and education. In a political climate where anti-immigration sentiment is on the rise, bringing with it renewed versions of old racist ideology and scapegoating, we would make sure that the issues arising from this dynamic are explored in discussion about institutional racism.

Changing sociopolitical dynamics also impact on students' sense of identity and their struggles to construct both new extended-group and intergroup relationships. The shift from a Black-White axis to a more multidimensional one and the need for coalitions between various ethnic groups of color bring new challenges. So too does the development in the 1990s of an economically successful segment of people of color, and the emergence of individual people of color in high government, and academic positions who actively collude with the creation and maintenance of racist ideology and practices. The curriculum would have to incorporate these issues.

Changing sociopolitical dynamics of racism also influence White students' journey. When racist ideology increasingly insists that Whites are the targets and victims of civil rights legislation and policies, it is especially important that White students not only know what not to be, but also to comfortably know what to be. It is vital that they construct an ethnic/cultural identity of which they can be proud, while dismantling the socially constructed identity of whiteness and superiority created by racism. White students must also unpack their culture, and decide which elements to keep and which elements to discard. Heightened attention to these issues becomes necessary.

Modifying and Adding Activities

Decisions about activities must occur within the framework of the students' developmental journey that we want to spark and guide. Modify activities and create new ones while keeping intact the overall principles and goals of the course. Your choices will therefore depend on the specifics of your students' characteristics, developmental needs, and learning styles; the structural possibilities of your setting; and current issues. When we began, we borrowed and/or modified some activities from others and invented many of our own. Now, there are many more resources available with useful ideas. See, for example:

Carter, M., & Curtis, D. (1995). *Training teachers: A harvest of theory and practice.* Minneapolis: Redleaf Press.

Darder, A. (1991). *Culture and power in the classroom: A critical foundation for bicultural education.* New York: Macmillan.

Gay, G. (1994). *At the essence of learning: Multicultural education.* West Lafayette, IN: Kappa Delta Pi.

Katz, J. (1979). *White awareness: A handbook for anti-racism training.* Norman: University of Oklahoma Press.

Nieto, S. (1992). *Affirming diversity: The sociopolitical context of multicultural education.* New York: Longman.

Tatum, B. D. (in press) *Why are all the black kids sitting together in the cafeteria?* New York: Basic Books.

York, S. (1992). *Developing roots and wings: A trainer's guide to affirming culture in early childhood programs.* Minneapolis: Redleaf Press.

Remember, however, that someone else's idea for an activity is useful only if it matches the needs of your students—and that any existing activity can be modified to make a better match.

THE CHOICE TO ACT AS THE MISSION OF LIVING

In closing, we are reminded that when we first began to teach the class, making it our own was never really a conscious concern. Although we were well aware of the fact that we were not inventing anti-racism education and that we were using things that we had heard about and learned from others, still it never really occurred to us that what would evolve would be anything other than our own.

When the Mina Shaunessey Scholars grant gave us the opportunity to reflect on our work and write about our teaching, we never thought twice that the writing would be about anything other than our "own" course. That sense comes, we think, not from a need for individualistic ownership of the experience but instead from a sense of solidarity with those forces in the universe that compel people to represent themselves in this world, and in this life. It is a sense of oneness with the choice to act as the real mission of living. For as Franz Fanon so eloquently put it: "There comes a time when silence is dishonest. What matters is not to know the world, but to change it" (quoted in King, 1976, p. 234).

We hope you will share this sense with us.

References

Anderson, M., & Collins, P. H. (Eds.). (1995). *Race, class, and gender; An anthology.* Belmont, CA: Wadsworth.

Aptheker, H. (1993). *Anti-racism in U.S. history.* Westport, CT: Praeger.

BaFá BaFá, a cross culture simulation. (1977). Available from Simulation Training Institute, 218 Twelfth Street, Del Mar, CA 92014.

Barndt, J. (1991). *Dismantling racism: The continuing challenge to white America.* Minneapolis: Augsburg Press.

Carnoy, M. (1994). *Faded dreams: The politics and economics of race in America.* New York: Cambridge University Press.

Chase, A. (1975). *The legacy of Malthus: The social costs of the new scientific racism.* New York: Alfred A. Knopf.

Clark, K. (1963). *Prejudice and your child* (3rd ed.). Boston: Beacon.

Cross, W. E., Jr. (1991). *Shades of black: Diversity in African-American identity.* Philadelphia: Temple University Press.

Cross, W. E., Jr., Parham, T. A., & Helms, J. E. (1991). The stages of Black identity development: Nigrescence models. In R. Jones (Ed.), *Black psychology* (3rd ed.) (pp. 319–338). San Francisco: Cobb and Henry.

Crossroads (producer), & Ruehle, C. (director). (1996). *Ending racism: Working for a racism free 21st century* [Video]. Available from Crossroads Milwaukee, 2218 N. 36th Street, Milwaukee, WI 53208.

Darder, A. (1991). *Culture and power in the classroom: A critical foundation for bicultural education.* New York: Bergin & Garvey.

Davis, A. Y. (1983). *Women, race & class.* New York: Vintage.

Dennis, R. (1981). Socialization and racism: The white experience. In B. Bowser & R. Hunt (Eds.), *Impacts of racism on white Americans* (pp. 71–86). Beverly Hills: Sage.

Derman-Sparks, L., & the ABC Task Force. (1989). *Anti-bias curriculum: Tools for empowering young children.* Washington, DC: NAEYC.

Derman-Sparks, L., Higa, C. T., & Sparks, B. (1980). Children, race and racism: How race awareness develops. *Interracial Books for Children Bulletin, 11*(3 & 4), 3–9.

Dominelli, A. (1992). An uncaring profession? An examination of racism in social work. In P. Braham, A. Rattansi, & R. Skellington (Eds.), *Racism and antiracism: Inequalities, opportunities, and policies* (pp. 164–178). London: Sage.

Du Bois, W. E. B. (1903). *The souls of black folk.* Chicago: A. C. McClurg.

Du Bois, W. E. B. (1985). *Against racism: Unpublished essays and papers, 1887–1961.* (H. Aptheker, Ed.). Amherst: University of Massachusetts Press.

Echevarria, W., Van Lennep, E., & Rivera, P. (Producers), & Leppzer, R. (director). (1992). *Columbus didn't discover us* [Film]. Wendall, MA: Turning Tide Productions.

Fanon, F. (1967a). *Black skins, white masks.* New York: Grove Press.

Fanon, F. (1967b). *A dying colonialism.* New York: Grove Press.

Foner, P. (Ed.). (1945). *Frederick Douglass: Selections from his writings.* New York: International Publishers.

Frammolino, R., Gladstone, M., & Wallace, A. (1996, March 16). Some regents seek UCLA admissions priority for friends. *The Los Angeles Times,* pp. A1, A18.

Frankenberg, R. (1993). *White women, race matters: The social construction of whiteness.* Minneapolis: University of Minnesota Press.

Franklin, J. H. (1993). *The color line: Legacy for the twenty-first century.* Columbia: University of Missouri Press.

Freire, P. (1970). *Pedagogy of the oppressed.* New York: Continuum.

Galen, G., with Palmer, T. (1994, January 31). White, male and worried. *Business Week,* p. 52.

Garcia, E., & McLauglin, B. (Eds.). (1995). *Meeting the challenge of linguistic and cultural diversity in early childhood education.* New York: Teachers College Press.

Gossett, T. F. (1963). *Race: The history of an idea in America.* New York: Schocken Books.

Gould, S. J. (1981). *The mismeasure of man.* New York: Norton.

Gould, S. J. (1995, February). Ghosts of bell curves past. *Natural History, 104*(2), 12–19.

Guthrie, R. V. (1976). *Even the rat was white: A historical view of psychology.* New York: Harper & Row.

Hardiman, R. (1979). *White identity development: A process oriented model for describing the racial consciousness of White Americans.* Unpublished doctoral dissertation, University of Massachusetts, Amherst.

Helms, J. E. (1984). Toward a theoretical explanation of the effects of race on counseling: A black and white model. *The Counseling Psychologist, 12*(4), 153–165.

Helms, J. E. (1990). Toward a model of white racial identity development. In J. E. Helms (Ed.), *Black and white racial identity: Theory, research and practice.* Westport, CT: Greenwood Press, pp. 49–66.

Herrnstein, R., & Murray, C. (1994). *The bell curve: Intelligence & class structure in American life.* New York: Free Press.

Hilliard, A. (1992, January). *Racism: Its origins and how it works.* Paper presented at the meeting of the Mid-West Association for the Education of Young Children, Madison, WI.

Hilliard, A. (1995). *The Maroon within us: Selected essays on African American community socialization.* Baltimore: Black Classic Press.

Hilliard, A. G., III, Jenkins, Y., & Scott, M. (1979). Behavioral criteria in research and the study of racism: Performing the jackal function (Technical Reports I, II, III, contract No. N00014–177–CO183). Washington, DC: Office of Naval Research.

hooks, b. (1995). *Killing rage: ending racism.* New York: Holt.

Institute of Race Relations. (1982). *Roots of racism.* London: Author.

Jarrico, P. (producer), & Biberman, H. (director). (1951). *Salt of the earth* [Film].

Jordan, W. D. (1974). *The white man's burden: Historical origins of racism in the United States.* London: Oxford University Press.

Kamin, L. (1974). *The science and politics of I.Q.* New York: Wiley.

Katz, J. (1978). *White awareness: A handbook for anti-racism training.* Norman: University of Oklahoma Press.

Kendall, F. (1995). *Diversity in the classroom: New approaches to the education of young children* (rev. ed.). New York: Teachers College Press.

Kim, J. (1981). *Processes of Asian-American identity development.* Unpublished doctoral dissertation, University of Massachusetts, Amherst.

King, L. M. (1976). On the nature of a creative world: Toward a restoration of creativity in psychology. In L. M. King, V. J. Dixon, & W. W. Nobles (Eds.), *African philosophy: Assumption & paradigms for research on black persons* (pp. 223–234). Los Angeles: Fanon Research and Development Center.

Kluckhohn, F., & Strodbeck, F. (1961). *Variations in value orientation.* New York: Row, Peterson.

Ladson-Billings, G. (1994). *The dreamkeepers: Successful teachers of African American children.* San Francisco: Jossey-Bass.

Marable, M. (1995). *Beyond black and white: Transforming African-American politics.* New York: Verso.

Meier, T., & Brown, C. R. (1994). The color of inclusion. *Journal of Emotional and Behavioral Problems, 3*(3), 15–18.

Memmi, A. (1965). *The colonizer and the colonized.* Boston: Beacon Press.

Moraga, C., & Anyaldua, G. (1981). *This bridge called my back: Writings by radical women of color.* Watertown, MA: Persephone Press.

Oliver, M., & Shapiro, T. (1995). *Black wealth/white wealth: A new perspective on racial equality.* New York: Routledge.

Omi, M., & Winant, H. (1986). *Racial formation in the United States: From the 1960s to the 1990s.* New York: Routledge.

Palmer, H. (producer & director), & Cronin, S. (producer). (1996). *Teaching umoja: Simultaneous culture-centric approaches to education* [Video]. Available from Umoja Communications, 6255 West Sunset Blvd. #101–18, Los Angeles, CA 90028.

Pierce, C. M. (1980). Social trace contaminants: Subtle indicators of racism. In S. Withey, R. Abeles, & L. Erlbaum (Eds.), *Television and social behavior: Beyond violence and children* (pp. 249–257). Hillsdale, NJ: Erlbaum.

Ramirez, M., & Castaneda, A. (1974). *Cultural democracy: Bicognitive development and education.* New York: Academic Press.

Ramsey, P. G. (1987). *Teaching and learning in a diverse world.* New York: Teachers College Press.

Roediger, D. (1991). *The wages of whiteness: Race and the making of the American working class.* New York: Verso.

Ryan, W. (1976). *Blaming the victim* (rev. ed.). New York: Vintage Books.

Sleeter, C. (1995). An analysis of the critique of multicultural education. In J. Banks & C. M. Banks (Eds.), *Handbook of research on multicultural education* (pp. 81–94). New York: Macmillan.

Smith, L. (1962). *Killers of the dream* (rev. ed.). New York: Norton. (Original work published 1949)

Stroup, N., & Fleming, J. (1995). *While we run this race: Confronting the power of racism in a Southern church.* Maryknoll, NY: Orbis Press.

Takaki, R. (1993). *A different mirror: A history of multicultural America.* Boston: Little, Brown & Company.

Tatum, B. D. (1992). Talking about race, learning about racism: The application of racial identity development theory in the classroom. *Harvard Educational Review, 62*(1), 1–24.

Tatum, B. D. (1995, February). *Stages of racial/ethnic identity development in the United States.* Paper presented at the meeting of the National Association for Multicultural Education, Washington, DC.

Terry, R. (1975). *For whites only* (rev. ed.). Grand Rapids, MI: Eerdmans.

Tucker, W. (1994). *The science and politics of racial research.* Urbana: University of Illinois Press.

Wellman, D. (1977). *Portraits of white racism.* New York: Cambridge University Press.

Yamada, M. (1976). *Camp notes and other poems.* San Francisco: Shameless Hussy Press.

Zinn, H. (1980). *A people's history of the United States.* New York: Harper and Row.

Index

About the Authors

CAROL BRUNSON PHILLIPS is Executive Director of the Council for Early Childhood Professional Recognition in Washington, DC. The Council serves as the home of the Child Development Associate National Credentialing Program, as well as the Head Start Fellows Program. Dr. Phillips is also the liaison for the international exchange between the schools in Reggio Emilia, Italy, and the early childhood community in the United States.

Dr. Phillips received her B.A. in psychology from the University of Wisconsin, her M.Ed. in Early Childhood Education from Erikson Institute, and her Ph.D. in Education from Claremont Graduate School. Dr. Phillips has been involved in the early childhood profession for many years. As a member of the Human Development Faculty at Pacific Oaks College in Pasadena, she specialized in early childhood education and cultural influences on development for 13 years.

LOUISE DERMAN-SPARKS is a long-time member of the Human Development Faculty at Pacific Oaks College in Pasadena and director of the Culturally Relevant/ Anti-Bias Education Leadership Project. She is also the senior author of *Anti-Bias Curriculum: Tools for Empowering Young Children*, published by the National Association for the Education of Young Children.

Professor Derman-Sparks received her B.A. in American literature and history from Brooklyn College and her M.A. in early childhood education from the University of Michigan. Beginning her career as a preschool teacher and childcare center director, she has taught adults for the past 23 years, and speaks and consults on anti-bias education nationally and internationally.